Time Out Guides Limited
Universal House
251 Tottenham Court Road
London W1T 7AB
Tel + 44 (0)20 7813 3000
Fax + 44 (0)20 7813 6001
Email guides@timeout.com
www.timeout.com

Editorial
Editors Jenny Landreth, Cath Phillips
Writer Jenny Landreth
Deputy Editor Anna Norman

Managing Director Peter Fiennes
Editorial Director Sarah Guy
Series Editor Cath Phillips
Business Manager Daniel Allen
Editorial Manager Holly Pick
Assistant Management Accountant
Ija Krasnikova

Design
Art Director Scott Moore
Art Editor Pinelope Kourmouzoglou
Senior Designer Henry Elphick
Graphic Designer Kei Ishimaru, Nicola Wilson

Picture Desk
Picture Editor Jael Marschner
Deputy Picture Editor Lynn Chambers
Picture Researcher Gemma Walters
Picture Desk Assistant Ben Rowe

Advertising
Commercial Director Mark Phillips

Marketing
Sales & Marketing Director North America
& Latin America Lisa Levinson
Senior Publishing Brand Manager Luthfa Begum
Art Director Anthony Huggins
Circulation & Distribution Manager Dan Collins
Marketing Intern Alana Benton

Production
Group Production Director Mark Lamond
Production Manager Brendan McKeown
Production Controller Damian Bennett

Time Out Group
Chairman Tony Elliott
Chief Executive Officer David King
Group Financial Director Paul Rakkar
Group General Manager/Director Nichola Coulthard
Time Out Communications Ltd MD David Pepper
Time Out International Ltd MD Cathy Runciman
Time Out Magazine Ltd Publisher/MD Mark Elliot
Group IT Director Simon Chappell
Marketing & Circulation Director Catherine Demajo

The Editors would like to thank Paul Akers, Bob Clark, Inna Costantini, Jo Hurst, Sue James, Britta Jaschinski, Dave McRoberts, Kevin Molloy, Chris Mullett, Valerie Selby, Graham Simmonds, Michael Tiritas, Steve Williams, Mr Woodcock and unknown individuals who gave directions or kindly conversed on some bleak cold days beside trees. And thanks particularly to Mark, Charlie and Izzy who always seemed willing to come along for the ride. Time Out would also like to thank Trees for Cities (020 7587 1320, www.treesforcities.org) for collaborating with us on this book with such enthusiasm.

Photography Britta Jaschinski.

Foreword

I cycle past St Pancras churchyard every working day of my life, yet it was only when I spotted a windswept group of prelates and parishioners one day that I paused to go inside. The Bishop of London was presiding over an event outside the small Norman church. It was as I wandered round the back of the building that I came across the Hardy Ash.

In the 1860s, the writer Thomas Hardy had been apprenticed to an architect, Arthur Blomfield, in Covent Garden. The building of the nearby Midland Railway had disrupted many of the graves in the churchyard and Hardy was tasked with making an inventory and reburying them. He stacked the headstones round a convenient ash tree. Then he seems to have moved on before the job was finished.

What remains is the scene he left, save for the extraordinary development of the tree, which has wrapped itself around the headstones as if to prevent anyone ever attempting to move them again. Each is numbered with a Roman numeral, and I like to think Hardy may have carved the numbers himself.

The Hardy Ash represents a wondrously direct and organic connection with history, but it is also the most beautiful artefact. When Trees for Cities asked me to nominate my favourite London tree for their Great Trees of London project, I chose it without hesitation. But, in truth, I do all the Great Trees, and so many more besides, a disservice. I love them all. And we need more, more for the greening of London, more to play their vital role in combating climate change. That's why I am passionate about the capital's fantastic arboreal heritage and proud to be a patron of Trees for Cities. We must keep planting!

Jon Snow
Patron, Trees for Cities

Contents

Introduction

Trees are in many ways the unsung heroes of our great city. From the street trees that turn London's busy thoroughfares into attractive boulevards, to the rich variety of trees that make up the capital's parks, squares, woodlands and gardens, trees are our constant friends, growing and blossoming in their own quiet way. The Victorians appreciated the vital role trees play in beautifying the city and cleaning the air, and their planting programme has given our generation a wonderful legacy – imagine how different Park Lane would be without its mature London planes that stand alongside the historic buildings as equal partners.

Trees for Cities is working to plant a new legacy for future generations, as well as helping to celebrate and protect London's existing tree heritage – and this book is an important part of that celebration. Trees for Cities started life as Trees for London in the early 1990s when a group of young Londoners came together around a shared vision for a new tree-planting programme that would match that of the Victorians. The charity was formed in 1993 with Charity Commission approval and initially funds were raised through club nights at some of London's leading nightlife venues. The first trees planted by the charity were a row of rowan trees on Westminster Bridge Road, which today help to make this very busy stretch of road more human and less polluted. This focus on dense urban areas of environmental and social need has characterised the charity's work ever since.

At the end of the 2008-09 season we planted our 145,000th tree. While the club nights that have over the years taken on a near-legendary status continue, the majority of the charity's funds are now raised from other sources: corporate sponsorships, individual giving schemes, the National Lottery, trusts and regeneration grants. And while tree-planting is still core to the charity's work, this is now complemented by other activities – creating community gardens on housing estates, vocational training for the long-term unemployed in arboriculture, horticulture and landscaping, an active programme of education with schools and community groups, putting on events such as the Tree-Athlon, and so on. With all these activities, particular attention is given to the young and people that can best be described as 'hard to reach', such as the long-term unemployed and those from ethnic minority backgrounds. In 2003 we celebrated our tenth anniversary with a change of name to Trees for Cities in response to requests for advice and support from cities around the world, and the charity now has projects in most major cities in England as well as in East Africa (Ethiopia and Kenya) and South America (Peru and Bolivia).

The Great Trees of London initiative grew out of the devastating Great Storm of 1987. To mark the storm's tenth anniversary in 1997, the tree officers for the London boroughs, the Government's Countryside Agency, and the *Evening Standard* rallied together and invited Londoners to nominate the capital's 'Great Trees'. To gain Great Tree status, a tree had to be publicly accessible (easily viewed from all sides) and to meet at least one of the following three criteria: historical significance (is the tree related to historical events or people, or does it have its own special story?); location (is the tree situated in a landmark location?); physical character (is the tree very large or old or an unusual shape?). All nominations were judged by an expert panel, and out of the first round of nominations, 41 trees were awarded Great Tree status and special plaques erected next to them. These included street trees such as the graceful Dorchester Plane; the less conspicuous but equally special strawberry tree in Battersea Park; and the historic Bexley Charter Oak.

A second round of nominations was opened to the public in 2008, to find a further 20 Great Trees, with a particular focus on inner London. This second phase has been generously supported by Barratt Homes, Magic 105.4, the Forestry Commission and the Royal Parks. The mix of historic trees, such as the Hardy Ash nominated by Jon Snow, and those trees that give a real sense of character to particular locations, such as the Tate Plane in the heart of Brixton, make these additional Great Trees all very special.

Of course, in reality, there are many more than 60 great trees in London, and I'm sure many people already have a favourite – for me, the century-old mountain ash that towers over the end of my garden in Clapham is a real source of calm, and gives great pleasure to my children through the tyre-swing hanging from one of its branches. However, the collection of trees in this book really are the capital's finest, and it's very exciting to see some of London's unsung heroes put on the podium and celebrated in all their glory.

Finally, I would like to say a big thank you to everyone who has contributed to the Great Trees of London initiative – from the project's sponsors, to the patrons of Trees for Cities, and figures such as Jon Snow, Neil Fox and Mayor Boris Johnson, who helped to promote it, to the judging panel and the many people who nominated trees. And, of course, a special thank you to Time Out for doing this book with us – I hope it will provide inspiration for all of us to do what we can to love and cherish the trees in our cities.

Graham Simmonds
Trustee, Trees for Cities, www.treesforcities.org

Introduction

I've been a London resident for longer than I haven't, and I thought I knew what I liked and didn't like in the city. But in researching this book, I discovered parts that were a complete mystery, parts I never thought I'd see, and parts I know I will never see again. The important thing has been to experience every Great Tree. You can't really begin to get the flavour without a good bit of standing and staring. Rain, wind and mud were involved – seeing trees is not the kind of thing you can do in a fashion sandal. On a bad day, it felt like traipsing; on a good one, like being given official dispensation to wander around. Some of the trees might generously be described as 'hard to love'; others leave a more immediate impact – and it's not always the most obvious ones that are the most affecting. But I have to report that whether it's been on a traffic roundabout on a rainy afternoon, or in glorious parkland in the spring sunshine, every single tree on this list bears viewing. And seeing them all has been a real privilege.

It's also been a privilege to talk to some of the many people involved in the care and management of London's trees. Committed to a fault, they shared their expertise and time without a quibble, and for that, I give thanks. We should all give thanks, actually, because they're often doing much more than their job; they're passionate advocates and it's down to them that London remains green, and will hopefully get greener.

You see a lot of other things when you're looking for trees – hidden passages, little doors in the oddest places, quirky rooftops. Not just grand buildings but day-to-day architecture. You see the way the city fits together, the way things can surprise you even in streets you've walked down hundreds of times. Notably, everywhere you go, there are little dots and dashes of green, from tiny slices of park grass, to wafty plants high on roof gardens. One of the benefits of writing this book is a new habit: wherever I go I'm constantly looking up, at the size, shape and type of tree I can see in passing. It's a great thing to do in a city, to look up – you see so much more. It connects you with London on different levels, it revives you and it definitely makes you glad to be here.

Jenny Landreth
Editor and author, The Great Trees of London

Central

The Berkeley Plane

Platanus x hispanica

The Berkeley Plane moves us into the tree equivalent of the Hollywood blockbuster. This is not about girth, height, rarity. This is about the whole picture. Because this tree, this not-so-humble plane, could be the most valuable tree in London, worth a cool three-quarters of a million quid for a bit of wood and a few leaves. Broken wood at that – it's lost a major lower limb, leaving it with a wonky eye-patch look.

Halfway between Oxford Street and Piccadilly, famous Berkeley Square is a landmark of classic London. Simply designed and well maintained, it's an oasis of huge plane trees and paths, offering a chance to remove the blinkers of built-up streets and look upwards. Given its Mayfair location, it's surprisingly unfussy, low-key and calm. Unlike some private squares in London, where a thick border of high shrubs makes a peep inside impossible, this public space can be easily viewed from the roads around, being penned-in only by short railings. Filled with huge urns and commemorative benches, it's a lovely spot in which to recover your nerves after the traffic-dodging required to get in. A listed pump house takes centre-stage, and a mix of new and old sculpture is dotted about the square, most notably the 1858 nymph by Pre-Raphelite sculptor Alexander Munro, which kindly doubles as a drinking fountain. The square gently slopes from north to south, and our selected tree is in the bottom south-west corner.

All the 30 or so planes in the square were planted by a local resident in 1789. At more than 200 years old, this plane's trunk has become fat and crumpled, its branches swooping upwards with statesman-like vigour. Many of the Berkeley Square planes share a feature: their trunks swell for a few feet before they bifurcate (that is, split into two). Bifurcation is a good look, open and inviting. Our tree, being Great, goes one step further, splitting into three. In the way big noses might suggest a family line, so this similarity suggests these trees are from the same family. That possibility is being turned into a definite in current tree management: new stock is being grown on from cuttings from these trees, to perpetuate the characteristics.

Back to the money. Who has declared that this tree is so valuable, and why? As developments gobble up greenery, the London Tree Officers Association has devised a system of valuation, to stop trees being seen as disposable commodities but as assets instead. Snappily known as CAVAT – the Capital Asset Value for Amenity Trees – this system takes into account the location, history, age and health of the tree, as well as the number of people who enjoy it, either as residents or visitors. This tree is so valuable because of its unparalleled high scoring in all these factors. Of course, it doesn't mean you can buy this tree for cash. It's valuable, not expensive. And each tree we see makes a contribution to the environment – so in that sense, this one may be exceptional, but it's no exception.

GETTING THERE

Map ❶

Location South-west corner of Berkeley Square, Mayfair, W1J 5AX.
Access The square is open from dawn to dusk.
Transport Green Park or Bond Street tube.
Directions Exit Green Park station on the north side of Piccadilly. Follow Stratton Street as it bends right, and turn left on to Berkeley Street. Berkeley Square is straight ahead, with the tree in the south-west corner, just behind a row of benches.

Species watch London Plane

Plane trees may be ubiquitous in the city, but they still stand proud.

If ever a disease strikes the London plane, or they reach the end of their lifespan, the capital's landscape will be absolutely decimated. They form a good half of our tree population. They're not a British native – *Platanus x hispanica* is believed to be a hybrid between the Oriental plane (*Platanus orientalis*) and the American plane (*Platanus occidentalis*), but as they may have been 'discovered' by John Tradescant in his botanical garden in Vauxhall, south London, their use in London makes some historical sense.

The London plane's ubiquity is mostly due to its distinctive properties. Its ability to deal with city pollution is unequalled, and it would have been planted en masse at a time when London air was appalling – thick and black with sooty smoke. Its success is down to the huge shiny leaves, which are easily washed clean by the rain, and the bark, which renews itself by peeling off in large chunks.

That means the pores never get clogged by grime, and give it a characteristic patched grey, cream, olive-green look, like protective camouflage. The tree survives in most soils, and can withstand heavy pruning and restricted root space. The seeds are sterile, so it doesn't make a nuisance of itself self-seeding everywhere; the tree is propagated by cuttings – which means that many of the London planes in the city are from the same stock, and therefore show similar growing patterns. The bristly brown fruits stay on the tree, which is less of a nuisance to people and parked cars.

Can something so useful actually be good-looking too? Yes, it can. The plane is stately and tall, giving a good dappled shade in full leaf; most of London's squares are full of them and, although the trees are common, they still line key roads – along Hyde Park, for instance – with a great sense of importance and dignity.

The Berkeley Plane

The St James's Indian Bean Tree

Catalpa bignonioides

We're on a famous busy main road, taxis to the left of us, taxis to the right; the nearest hotel is the Ritz, the nearest 'supermarket' Fortnum & Mason. A thin strip of sky is visible between the rampant heights of abundant neo-classical buildings. Behind some black railings is the only small breathing space in the immediate vicinity: the churchyard of the Wren-designed St James's. At the front of it is our tree, tired and slumped in the middle of a hive of conspicuous consumption.

The tree is in its third act, moving towards the end. It has been propped up once, and now appears to need more than a shoulder to lean on. Planted in 1928, it has already well outlived its supposed 60-year lifespan. Fortunately, it's in the care of members of the St James's community, who are nurturing seedlings from the tree in their own gardens – understudy babies growing in the wings should it decide to give up permanently. The main trunk, cracked and dry, leans away from the railings, with one branch heading back to poke through the wrought ironwork above the gate, as if for support. All this fatigue makes the tree look a little precarious, almost resting on the striped plastic roofs of the covered arts and crafts market surrounding it in the courtyard.

The *Catalpa* is sometimes known as the canopy tree, because the huge leaves offer great shade. The idea of a humble natural refuge chimes well with a churchyard setting, but it's hard to get much of an actual sense of that because of the market tarpaulins around it. Or it may be that it was planted to be a blowsy show-off, because this tree can carry that off very well. The Indian bean tree is Indian in the Native American sense, and bean in the sense that it dangles with long pods, which start off resembling enlongated hanging green caterpillars and turn black-purple in autumn. The leaves are flopsy, huge and plentiful: their weight can bring lower branches right down. It flowers in summer with huge white upright panicles, followed by the bean pods, which can remain on the tree through the winter.

St James's Church was designed by Sir Christopher Wren, and is his only surviving West End church; it even survived being bombed in World War II. Its current post-war roof features solar panels, marking it out as a progressive listed building. Indeed, it has a reputation as being a liberal church, replacing the word 'congregation' with 'community', for instance, to underline the pastoral commitment. The classic churchyard elements – the statuary of cherubims and headstones, the twisting ivy and the higgledy-piggledy paving slabs – combine with the unusual, such as the counselling caravan. The only jarring member of the 'community' is a reproachful ceramic owl on the tree, fixed with an unconvincing glare to ward off pigeons.

GETTING THERE

Map ❷

Location St James's churchyard, 197 Piccadilly, W1J 9LL.
Access The churchyard is open from 8am to 6pm – later if there's an event at the church.
Transport Piccadilly Circus tube/ 9, 14, 19, 22, 38 bus.
Directions Leave the station by the 'Piccadilly (South Side)' exit. At the top of the stairs, bear left down Piccadilly. When you reach St James's Church, walk through the iron gates. The Indian bean is immediately to the right.

The Dorchester Plane

Platanus x hispanica

The tree outside the Dorchester hotel is just a tree in the sense that the Dorchester is just a hotel. You don't have to know much about either trees or hotels to recognise an understatement here: the Dorchester is a famously great hotel, and the tree outside it is officially a Great Tree of London.

The tree sits right on the edge of the Dorchester's land, bursting out of a small front garden that has been landscaped as if it were much larger. The planting around it is unimaginative, with the kind of clean precision that suggests stray leaves are regularly vacuumed up. Against the base of the trunk there's a tiny brown house; play 'guess who lives there' if you're spinning a yarn to a child, but it's just a tarted-up electricity box. If you look closely on a summer's day, you can see thick black cables snaking up to a number of bare round bulbs hidden by the leaves. But stand back, and wait a few months! Because it's on leafless nights that this tree becomes the true landmark that it is. Throughout autumn and winter, its heavy branches head for the sky hung with hundreds of lightbulbs, like reachable stars in a night sky only ever properly dark in the middle of a thunderstorm (this being over-lit central London). It's then that this tree becomes an evocative sight, a romantic one even, to match the romance of the hotel's glamorous history.

Part of the appeal of the tree lies in its location: a humble tree, in its natural form, beside the opulent wealth of the hotel. It's a clever contrast, simply contrived. You might imagine that the Dorchester would decorate itself exotically. But this is a London plane planted to one side of an avenue of planes, a majestic streak of green through the middle of the six-lane traffic of Park Lane, which divides the huge edifices of magnificent buildings on one side from Hyde Park on the other. Common London planes may be, but their trunks are never dull and uniform because of their unique shedding pattern; this one has a gruff trunk in a crumpled, un-shed state that is as rewarding a sight as dry old skin. It was planted around the time that the Dorchester became a hotel, in the early 1930s, and has the stately form and perfectly erect shape of a tree knowing it has to hold itself in for the cameras.

The absolutely best way to see this tree is coming out of the revolving doors of the Dorchester (head here for afternoon tea if you can't afford one of the fabulous suites). Raise your gaze and enjoy the plane's perfect shape, a dark umbrella against the frequently grey London skyline.

GETTING THERE

Map ❸

Location Outside the Dorchester hotel, Park Lane, Mayfair, W1K 1QA.
Access On a public road and accessible at all times.
Transport Hyde Park Corner tube/ 2, 10, 36, 73, 137, 148, 436 bus.
Directions Leave Hyde Park Corner station by exit 2, and take the Park Lane subway. The Dorchester is a few minutes' walk north on Park Lane, on the right-hand side.

The Brunswick Plane

Platanus x hispanica

Roll up, roll up, something for all the family: an inspiring tree in a full and rich location. There's a fantastic strand of social history in Brunswick Square, and a lovely adjoining children's playground, which you can enter only in the tow of a child. The playground is called Coram's Fields and, together with the square, it formed the original grounds of the Foundling Hospital set up by philanthropic sea captain Thomas Coram in 1739. The word 'hospital' at that time was extracted from 'hospitality' rather than being a medical term; Coram was appalled at the sight of abandoned and dying babies and children on the streets of the city, and worked tirelessly in his retirement to create the Foundling Hospital specifically for these vulnerable, deserted children. They were brought here in their droves; in four years, nearly 15,000 children were presented at the hospital's doors. Coram's extraordinary act of benevolence has continued to inspire works of fiction, and the Foundling Museum on the same site, as well as documenting a harsh side of London's history, shows how he also inspired his contemporaries, including Handel and Hogarth, to become involved.

The current layout of Brunswick Square is the same as it was in the 19th century, and its purpose as a respite for city dwellers hasn't changed either. It isn't fancy, but it is effective. As with many of the city's squares, the original railings were requisitioned in World War II, and have been replaced. That quite a few London planes have made Great Tree status isn't surprising, as there are so many in the capital. But this one looks different. It really is great, and should be Grade-II listed, like the square in which it lives. The trunk has a huge girth; from about three foot above the ground, it resembles bad Christmas wrapping, all swollen and lumped together; from the top of that the major branches split off. The base of the trunk has very defined buttress roots, which can make you believe you're looking at the top of a monumental root system, reaching down as far as the tree reaches up.

But what makes this tree really stand out is, first, its low branches and, second, the spread of those branches. They are rare in such a setting; this has always been a recreational park, and it's a joy that they haven't been pruned at the behest of Health & Safety. Long, thin branches twist and turn, like arthritic-jointed arms reaching out from the tree; not thick, but strong, dipping towards the ground but not quite touching it. They're tempting too – sitting on a branch, even a low one, is almost a requirement if an opportunity presents itself. But these contorted branches do have a sense of fragility, even as, lean-muscled, they gloriously hold themselves up and out.

GETTING THERE

Map ❹

Location Brunswick Square, Hunter Street, Bloomsbury, WC1.
Access The square is open from 7.30am to dusk.
Transport Russell Square tube/ 59, 68, 91, 168 bus.
Directions Turn right out of Russell Square station, and left at the roundabout. The square is opposite the Renoir cinema side of the Brunswick Centre, with the plane situated roughly in the centre.

The Abbey Plane

Platanus x hispanica

The Abbey Plane is quite lovely, but not necessarily breathtaking on its own – it definitely borrows from its unrivalled location in Dean's Yard, beside Westminster Abbey. Whether you're a royal worshipper, a rampant atheist or somewhere in between, the tree is a great excuse to go beyond a façade familiar from postcards and news items and discover a couple of delightful green gems.

Dean's Yard is a gated quadrangle a few steps from the Houses of Parliament and the associated bustle of tourists and politicians. Head past the wooden security cabin, and it feels like you're in a different time and place, even if you can still hear the traffic. Here lies a large green with trees on the boundary, surrounded on all sides by the Abbey and associated buildings, mostly church or school-related – Westminster School has been on the site since the 12th century. At that time, the green would have been covered with crops and animals, as this was part of the Abbey's farm, worked by the monks; today, it's a playing field for privileged boys. Our tree is on the left as you enter the quad, and though there are other planes on the green, this one is the most distinguished: you'll know you have the right one if it has a bit of pipe sticking out. Yes, a pristine historical setting – a UNESCO World Heritage Site, no less – and a Great Tree… with a bit of pipe sticking out. Its trunk has grown to kindly accommodate a free-standing piece of vertical drainpipe that would have stood at the edge of the grass until it was swallowed up, creating a rather strange effect.

This could almost be an *orientalis* plane; the growth of the trunk would support that. It's broader at the base, almost triangular, not as straight-up as the other planes in the grounds. It also has a beautifully textured trunk, as gorgeously tactile as a piece of old felted fabric, as nobbly as a warty old troll.

When you visit the tree, it's worth veering left, through the Abbey, to find College Garden, thought to be England's oldest garden, where the medieval monks grew medicinal herbs and veg. It's now a beautifully maintained and sizeable plot, a large lawn dominated by plane trees endowed by Queen Victoria in the 1850s, ringed with well-shaped evergreens, ornamental trees, statuary and a knot garden. To get to it, you have to go through a dark stone walkway, memorials underfoot; halfway along, the walkway opens on one side to reveal, through high arches, the stunning Little Cloister Garden, a film-set of a garden. A tiny, enclosed courtyard in the heart of the buildings, it features a perfect stone fountain, clipped box balls, aromatic plants – hell, even the daisies in the lawn look designed. It provides a sense of peace and contemplation, but, alas, you can only look through ornate railings.

Before you leave, take a second to imagine this place on a winter's night – dark, frosted, eerily lit, the traffic and choir practice silenced, with the only noise coming from Big Ben on the hour, sounding out as it has done for the past 150 years.

GETTING THERE

Map ❺

Location Dean's Yard, Westminster Abbey, Westminster, SW1P 3PA.
Access Dean's Yard is open to the public during daylight hours. The College Garden is open 10am to dusk, though days may vary.
Transport St James's Park or Westminster tube.
Directions Follow signs to Westminster Abbey from either station. The entrance to Dean's Yard is through the stone gateway to the right of the Abbey. The tree is located on the immediate left as you enter.

The Embankment Plane

Platanus orientalis

The Victoria Embankment has purpose. We can pontificate about what it brings to the city; how it's a beautiful broad avenue following the north side of the river, that gentle curve of the Thames running from Westminster to Blackfriars Bridge, with great historic buildings such as Somerset House and Banqueting House lying behind it. We can date the planting of the Embankment Plane by the building of this street, from 1864 to 1870. But the purpose of building it, this feat of civil engineering, is where the stuff of life comes in: it was created to house London's sewerage system. Shit happens – thanks to Victorian engineer Joseph Bazalgette, we just don't have to see much of it.

The Embankment Plane is one of hundreds of planes planted at 20-feet intervals all along the street. This one is on the corner of Horse Guards Avenue, on the edge of Victoria Embankment Gardens. Given that the trees were likely planted on landfill – not the best growing matter – they're doing pretty well. The landfill might go some way to account for their varied growth patterns, although it may also be that along the Embankment there are different species from the same genus. This particular plane, like half a dozen others along this stretch, veers more towards the oriental side of the family: more *Platanus orientalis* than *Platanus x hispanica*. It has a smoother bark, and a different crown structure – more compact, with a lighter canopy of limbs – than its more common brethren. Although its leaves are fingered in the same way as the *hispanica*, the fingers are more distinctly tapered and delicate. But examples of *Platanus orientalis* are rare, and it's a distinction that can be hard to call when the provenance of the trees is hidden by time.

Looking from the south side, the trees form a screen to the buildings behind, but they are also an integral part of a highly detailed, well-decorated urban space. Even the dolphin-entwined lamps and sphinx-armed benches have significance. The more obvious stars of the Embankment might be the Cleopatra's Needle obelisk, a gift to the British from the viceroy of Egypt, which was erected in 1878, and the gold eagle of the Royal Air Force Memorial, unveiled in 1923. But, as in so much of London, the area is like good panto: it's always worth looking behind you! There, you'll find Victoria Embankment Gardens: a gorgeous wedge of city greenery of some scope, and with some lovely specimen trees. As well as being much used by tourists and lunching workers on warm days, it's been a popular place for commemorative statues – even Bazalgette gets one. One of the most historic structures in the area is the York Water Gate, dating from the 1620s. An ornate Italianate entrance, it once led from York House mansion down to the river, but the building of the Embankment caused the Thames to be narrowed, and so the gate became landlocked and is now marooned on the other side of the gardens. You can stand by it and visualise an older time; then sniff the air, and give thanks for progress and sewers.

GETTING THERE

Map 6

Location On the north side of Horse Guards Avenue, at the junction with Victoria Embankment, Westminster, SW1.

Access On a public road and accessible at all times.

Transport Embankment or Westminster tube.

Directions From Embankment station, turn right and walk along the river; Horse Guards Avenue is the second road on the right. From Westminster station in the other direction, turn left and the road is the third on the left.

The Gower Plane 🍁

Platanus x hispanica

Don't be put off by artist and writer John Ruskin, who described Gower Street as the depth of street architecture. Your first look at the Gower Plane might not exactly light up the sky either. But if the street doesn't grow on you, the tree might, with a bit of help from context.

There are a few attractive green squares in the Gower Street area – Bedford, Russell, Gordon – but the street itself is quite a blank. It's long and straight, with three lanes of one-way traffic, and even though it's lined with a row of flat-fronted Georgian houses, their blue plaques noting the history within, they have been made filthy by the London air. As the area around Gower Street contains such impressive buildings as the British Museum, you can begin to see what Ruskin meant. This must be the journey, not the destination.

The Gower Plane is equally 'so-what'. It's lonely and not in a conducive setting; cramped, in reduced light, with few available nutrients. Stare at it long enough and you might grudgingly conclude that its trunk is… a bit curved. But behind a rather ordinary tree lie some interesting snippets of history.

For instance, obliquely, we have the French to thank for our street trees, at least in their quantity. When Paris was remodelled by civic planner Baron Georges-Eugène Haussmann in the 1850s, he destroyed a lot of the medieval city to create the famous tree-lined boulevards. The Victorians were influenced by that – you only have to look at Victoria Embankment to see how far – and began to plant up the streets of London in the 1860s and '70s. By the end of the century it was common practice, and documents from the time show a clear understanding of good tree management. And though wealthy Victorians were renowned for travelling abroad for exotic species, London's Metropolitan Board of Works would have had a very limited palette of species to plant from.

Our tree is not that old, and links in to a more contemporary understanding of the urban landscape. It's one thing having a view of tree tops from afar, and entirely another having the tree itself. This one is at a crossroads, at the end of a row of trees in Torrington Place. It's a strong visual link: it breaks up Gower Street, tells you where Torrington Place is, and so serves as a way-finder, an indicator of distance, a link from one place to another. It has literally been planted as a landmark, an example of the way roadway design can work for street users.

If social history and urban design concepts aren't enough, take a look at the building next to the tree. Grade-I listed and currently a Waterstone's bookshop, it's an elaborately flamboyant piece of decorative architecture, in a Flemish-Franco Gothic style. It was designed in 1908 by Charles Fitzroy Doll, who also created the nearby towering terracotta extravaganza, the Hotel Russell, based on the Château de Madrid in the Bois de Bologne. Which brings us neatly back to Paris again.

GETTING THERE

Map ❼

Location Outside Waterstone's bookshop, at the corner of Torrington Place and Gower Street, Fitzrovia, WC1E 6EQ.
Access On a public road and accessible at all times.
Transport Goodge Street tube/ 10, 73, 390 bus.
Directions From the station, head across Tottenham Court Road, and down Chenies Street. Turn left at Gower Street; the plane is on the right at the traffic lights.

The Marylebone Elm

Ulmus x hollandica 'Vegeta'

This tree is a survivor, twice over. Strike one: the tree stands at the top end of Marylebone High Street, a strong-armed stone's throw from glorious Regent's Park. It would probably have started urban life as part of the landscaping in the parish church of St Marylebone. But it now finds itself hailing a cab on the pavement outside a small Garden of Rest, built in 1952 on the site a former church. The church was so severely damaged by World War II air raids it had to be demolished in 1949, but our tree survived the bombing.

Strike two: Dutch Elm Disease (DED) stalked the world in the late 1960s and '70s. It's not over-dramatic to call it a global disaster: it decimated the treescape of Europe and North America, destroying tens of millions of trees (Australia escaped because of its geographical isolation). DED killed more than 20 million trees in the UK, about three-quarters of the elm population. Britain was changed irrevocably by one accidentally imported micro-fungus.

However, this Huntingdon elm survived! And it did so in good health – it has a strong grey trunk, with thin, even ridges weaving neatly upwards. The cultivar is a vigorous grower, up rather than across, and this one has managed over 100 feet in an estimated 150 years. The domed crown opens out way above the nearby buildings, and stretches itself across the street. As the leaves yellow in autumn, it becomes an oversized Belisha beacon. For a while the only elm in Westminster, it has lost its claim to that position with the planting of a new, disease-resistant variety, the 'New Horizon'. The planting of new elms in London is welcomed; diversity of species encourages wildlife, and is good for tree management. It ensures that great swathes of trees won't be lost through one disease again. And it's cheaper to maintain a spread of different species because they don't all need the same thing at the same time – like suddenly having an elderly population all of whom needed hip replacements.

Think about diversity while you sit in the Garden of Rest, or you could hum 'Hark the Herald Angels Sing', in homage to its composer Charles Wesley, who has an obelisk-shaped memorial here. The Garden is a discreet and peaceful semi-circle constructed from York stone, gravel and planting. Ancient gravestones line the walls and carved plaques tell the story of the old parish church. It has a couple of trees of its own – an Indian Bean and a Judas tree – the latter surely planted for its delightful summer flowers rather than its common name, given the context. Neither are particularly impressive specimens: not survivors, like our elm. So when you're done with considering diversity, it's also worth reflecting for a moment on the nature of survival.

GETTING THERE

Map ❽

Location At the northern end of Marylebone High Street, Marylebone, W1.
Access On a public road and accessible at all times. The Garden of Rest is open from dawn to dusk.
Transport Baker Street or Regent's Park tube/18, 27, 30, 205, 453 bus.
Directions From Regent's Park station, turn left (right from Baker Street), then walk along Marylebone Road. Turn down Marylebone High Street. Go past the Conran Shop; the elm is on the right, next to a zebra crossing and just before the Sixty 6 furniture/clothes shop.

The Cheapside Plane

Platanus x hispanica

To be a true Cockney, you have to be born within the sound of Bow bells – which makes our tree a proper Londoner, because the bells, from the church of St Mary-le-Bow, are just across the street. The tree is located at the junction of Wood Street and Cheapside, and its survival is something to be celebrated, not least by the buildings next door. The tree's protected status extends to the low buildings directly beside it, which are forbidden from getting any higher in order to preserve the tree. In an area absolutely rife with modern development, this historic plane is protecting these 18th-century buildings from rapacious developers.

The tree, which is at least 250 years old, is possibly the oldest tree in the Square Mile, an area that goes right to the heart of London history. For more than 1,000 years, Cheapside has been a busy thoroughfare; it was one of the earliest market sites, and the nearby streets (Milk Street, Honey Lane, Bread Street, Poultry) are named after the goods sold on them. The plane stands on the site of the churchyard of St Peter's, which was destroyed by the Great Fire of London in 1666; a second great fire ripped through this area in 1940, and our tree survived that too. It also survived a direct bomb hit during World War II.

The tree served a useful life as a place to tie up the horses while men went to work in the banks. And as well as being at the heart of commerce, it is a tree surrounded by literary connections. Wordsworth lived nearby and in 1797 wrote 'The Reverie of Poor Susan' about the area. Dickens talked about the pollution of Cheapside in *Great Expectations*. The tree famously housed families of rooks until they fled for greener pastures, as detailed by Walter Thornbury in 1878: 'How pleasantly on a summer morning that last of the Mohicans, the green plane-tree now deserted by the rooks, at the corner of Wood Street, flutters its leaves!' He's referencing the famous novel of 1826, and it's nice to think that this simple Cockney plane was inspiring literary allusions way back.

And now? With a history of that pedigree, surely our tree's grandeur must be recognised today? Actually, no. Alongside developments waging a war for space, the tree stands in a tiny dark square behind some black railings; it reaches high above the low shops. The trunk looks old but not tired, standing straight and strong. The square's view inwards is not attractive, with the backs of buildings on three sides, an ugly mix of blank windows, pipes and air-conditioning units. There are a couple of benches, and a meagre bit of planting. The incongruous addition of a couple of tree ferns does nothing to lift the sense of a damp hole; their leaves are above head height, so you see mainly brown woolly trunks. Some 150 years on, this plane still seems like the last of the Mohicans, and long may it be so.

GETTING THERE

Map ❾

Location On the corner of Cheapside and Wood Street, City of London, EC2V 7WS.
Access On a public road and accessible at all times.
Transport St Paul's tube/8, 25, 242 bus.
Directions From St Paul's station, head east along Cheapside (away from St Paul's Cathedral). The tree is on the left, just after Gutter Lane.

The Regent's Plane

Platanus x hispanica

If youth is wasted on the young, then Great Trees are definitely wasted on students. Form into study groups and discuss.

The Regent's Plane is in the grounds of the private Regent's College, so access is restricted. And as the route through the private areas is not straightforward, it may involve being escorted. The path takes you across a large courtyard, planted with careful drama, where expensively educated young Americans come to smoke. You come through to a large manicured lawn over which this plane presides – a pleasant open space planted with some huge, mostly very healthy trees, spaced along a path. These trees cleverly provide a visual link to those beyond in Regent's Park – lending one landscape to the other, and blurring the boundaries to expand the sense of space. It feels, on the one hand, quite vibrant, with newer additions such as a secret garden through the large shrubs behind the trees, and, on the other, quite rarified, probably because of the Regency buildings on both sides and on which even the ivy looks listed. These buildings have, in their glorious past, served as 'building doubles' on television programmes for more famous (and unavailable) locations. The college grounds are beautifully maintained, and are often the venue for conferences. Clearing the huge slippery plane leaves when they fall must be something of a task.

The tree in question sits in a little green island splitting a path. Its size is magnificent, its shape broadly columnar, its trunk very straight. It's always had enough space and light just to zoom on up ahead. The noticeable thing is that this tree has not been touched by the pruning saw. This is it, in all its unadulterated glory. It's related to the planes in Berkeley Square (*see p12*) – it might be from the same stock – and it's nice to imagine London gardeners of the time travelling from square to park with cart-loads of saplings. It's around 200 years old, dating from the days of John Nash, who planned a lot of villas around the park but built only eight; on maps from the 1830s, this is marked as South Villa. The trees were planted here to make residents feel like they were in the country, and when the park first opened in 1845, the public were allowed in only two days a week. It's ironic that this tree, however great, should have come full circle, and once again only be completely accessible to the privileged few.

GETTING THERE

Map ⑩

Location Regent's College, Inner Circle, Regent's Park, Westminster, NW1 4NS.
Access By arrangement only. During the week call the faculty manager (7487 7494); at weekends, the main reception (7487 7700).
Transport Baker Street tube/ 18, 27, 30, 205 bus.
Directions Take the Marylebone Road exit from the station and turn left. After Madame Tussauds, turn left at York Gate and cross the bridge. Follow the road into the Regent's College main entrance, and report to reception.

The Regent's Plane

Pollarding

A necessary pruning method for trees in today's space-lacking cities.

London is full of pollarded trees; they are very distinctive-looking, but not pleasing to every eye, in the way that one man's modern architecture is another man's carbuncle. Pollards have been heftily pruned to look as if they have cartoon-like club ends to their branches, with hundreds of thin shoots coming out from a bulging blob, instead of the natural shape of delicate tapering branches. They are generally just managing to put out a few leaves when everything else around them is fully greened, compounding the look that they have suffered a tragic accident. Deformed lollipops with flapping mould. So why do we choose to uglify our trees?

Pollarding is a way of pruning a tree by cutting back the head of main branches, in order to restrict height, and concentrate the growth of foliage out, rather than up. It used to be the method of keeping trees low and productive, as it brings new wood every year. It's undertaken now to maintain a tree's shape given the planting conditions – which is why we see pollarded trees on main roads or in residential areas, where maintenance is more rigorous than for trees on open land, which have more room to grow.

Pollarding is actually beneficial to both people and trees. Leaving a tree in a natural state could result in overhanging branches pulling on overhead wires, blocking light, or being torn at by large lorries and buses, which can cause damage both to the tree, and to the person on whose head the broken-off branch falls.

Pollarding is best done in late winter or early spring, when there is plenty of food in the tree and it won't be under water stress. Only certain species are tolerant of pollarding, however; these include limes and London planes – common street trees – as well as other broad-leaved trees such as acer, oak, beech and hornbean. Once pollarding starts, you have to continue it, repruning every two to five years.

The Hardy Ash 🌿

Fraxinus excelsior

Put simply, this is a plain old ash tree. But you can't look at one piece of the jigsaw alone, you have to see every piece, building to a fantastic picture. From a bald start, it's superlatives all the way.

You can start your walk to the tree through the newly developed King's Cross/St Pancras area, wheeling out the old clichés about the conscious blend of old and new, art and architecture, gothic red brick versus contemporary glass slabs. Then you arrive at the railed-in space of St Pancras Old churchyard, surrounding what is possibly the oldest site of Christian worship in Britain. It's open and wide-pathed, with small areas of lawn; the kind of place that gives you breathing room. Packed with significant, intricate memorials, ornate bits of Victoriana and huge trees, it's as welcome as a sparkly old piece of costume jewellery in a stark modern collection.

Different bits of the jigsaw show how the site is significant to London. Dickens used this graveyard as a body-snatching location in *A Tale of Two Cities*. Mary Wollstonecraft, of *Frankenstein* fame, and her husband were first buried here, until their bodies were taken to Bournemouth. The John Soane mausoleum, designed by Soane for himself, his wife and their child, was inspiration for Sir Giles Gilbert Scott's traditional – now rare – red telephone box. Fast forward to the summer of 1968, and this was one of the sites where the Beatles had 'Mad Day Out' photos taken, modelling a full array of general groovy garishness.

Look up, and you'll see an ash tree surrounded by a low privet hedge, a very suburban, neatly trimmed circle around a good example of this British native. But if you feel a sense of disappointment at its ordinariness, then get closer, because the hedge is hiding a secret – it's a very clever piece of planting that allows this part of the picture to reveal itself bit by bit. Inside the hedge, right around the base of the tree, is a three-deep stack of old tombstones, with the trunk growing over them. It looks like the tree is moving to cover them in the way that a benign sea creature oozes over its suffocating prey. This has happened in the course of 250 years, though you get a sense that when you turn your back the tree moves surreptitiously forward, like some spooky arboricultural game of 'What's the time, Mr Wolf?' What's more, these tombstones weren't stacked by any old Victorian; author Thomas Hardy studied architecture in London in the 1860s, and when a new railway was being built through the churchyard, he got the unenviable job of exhuming the remains and moving the stones. It's surprising that the stones have never been moved. Maybe it became too poignant a task, and too potentially destructive to the tree.

Don't leave without viewing two extraordinary elms further down the path. If Tim Burton designed trees, these would be them. Grafts on to straight trunks have taken 'contorted' to extremes – they are now a gnarled, dark mass of branches resembling crazy hair; nature mutating until it's as mad as a basket of snakes.

GETTING THERE

Map ⑪

Location Churchyard of St Pancras Old Church, Pancras Road, Camden, NW1 1UL.

Access The churchyard is open from dawn to dusk.

Transport King's Cross tube/rail/ Mornington Crescent tube/346, 214 bus.

Directions From King's Cross station, take exit 4 or 5 on to Pancras Road and turn right. Walk alongside St Pancras International, then turn left, go under a bridge, and turn right on to Pancras Road again. The churchyard is another 300 feet on the right. The ash is at the back of the church.

West

The Fulham Palace Holm Oak

Quercus ilex

It's not fashionable, banishment, but if you were going to be banished, then Fulham, when it was a far-flung outpost of the capital, would have been quite nice. Fulham Palace was the country residence of various Bishops of London from the 11th century, but the lovely gardens of the estate owe their historical renown to one particular Bishop – Bishop Compton – banished here for two years in 1686 by King James II, for being anti-Catholic. During his years in disgrace, he paid particular attention to the grounds. He made the most of his job looking after the Church of England overseas, and sent missionaries to the States, notably Virginia, to collect rare plants for the Fulham acreage. So the gardens housed the first American magnolia and azalea, alongside a collection of unusual trees. Its trees remain magnificent and notable, none more so than the old oak flopped out in the corner.

The Fulham Palace HolmOak predates the garden's fame; it's around 500 years old, and was probably planted when the palace was built in 1495. It's less glamorous than some of the other species here, so is that rare thing: a celebrity of substance.

The lawns stretch out from the Grade-I listed building, dotted with glorious, upright trees. It's more than charming – it's splendid. Away from the glare of display, huddling quietly in the corner where the garden wall curves to an end, is our tree – not upright. A dark niche is a more characterful place to find this ancient treasure, an absolute gift for imaginative play.

The oak is probably the most recognisable of English trees, but while you'll find acorns on every species, if you're looking for the classic in-out wavy oak leaf on this tree, you won't find it. This is a *Quercus Ilex*, otherwise known as a holm or holly oak – holm being an ancient name for holly, *ilex* being the Latin name for the holly genus. *Quercus ilex* is the most common evergreen oak; it has rounded oval leaves that look like young holly leaves – glossy and dark green on top and with a whiter, felty underside. The younger leaves tend to be more toothed and spiny, probably to protect them from grazing animals. It also has catkins, the sweet name for the dangly male flower clusters. It's hard to say how tall the tree might have been, as height has ceased to be an issue. The centre of the original trunk has died, leaving an empty dip; around it, circling the mulchy void, the outer branches have become the new trunks. The huge, thick branches are splayed out, some running horizontal to the ground like heavy snakes. Around the dip, old roots protude, blackened, mournful and wizened like fingers in a gothic painting. Because of the tree's recumbent pose, the leaf cover creates a canopy under which to shelter; the tree has created it's own great den. Even in this old and knackered state, it still exudes solidity.

GETTING THERE

Map ⑫

Location Fulham Palace, Bishop's Avenue, Fulham, SW6 6EA.
Access The palace grounds are open from dawn to dusk.
Transport Putney Bridge tube/ 14, 39, 22, 74, 85 bus.
Directions It's a 20-minute walk from the station. Cross the Putney Bridge Approach road and go through the stone gates that lead to the left of the church and on to a red cycle path. The entrance to Fulham Palace is past the green iron gates on the right. The oak is on the other side of the palace, by the boundary wall.

The Fulham Palace Holm Oak

The Ravenscourt Plane

Platanus x hispanica

Anthropomorphism isn't restricted to Disney animals. The principle – the attribution of human characteristics to non-human things – can be applied to trees, and if animated mice can save the world, then casting a tree in a lead role is practically sane. And this tree is definitely a comedy character. Grumpy. Old. Eccentric. It looks like it has just poked its head above ground to have a moan about something. The lowest two branches resemble broken skinny arms waving in indignation, and from the top of the tree springs some screwy unkempt hair.

Enough whimsy… but this *is* a funny tree. For a start, it's very short and fat. It's as if someone who is all fingers and thumbs has tried to mould a triangle out of mashed potato; the result is a huge trunk six feet in diameter, all wobbly and knobbled, but fabulously textural. The tree has grown out rather than up and has no major branches, instead possessing feeble, twisted limbs. All the energy has been directed to the trunk, but even this hasn't grown in a regular way – there's nothing straight about it. So this is an atypical specimen in a 32-acre park full of perfection. No wonder it's grumpy.

The 100-year-old tree stands as a focal point on the open grass area towards the south of Ravenscourt Park, whose history dates from medieval times. It was originally the grounds of a manor house, and the lake in the centre of the park is a remnant of the original moat fed by Stamford Brook. Only the stable block remains, now housing a café. In 1887 the grounds were sold for £58,000, and a year later a public park opened, laid out by Lieutenant Colonel JJ Sexby. As the Chief Officer of Parks for London County Council, Sexby had a hand in many of the capital's parks that date from that time – which is lots. Victorians took great pride in their open spaces, seeing them as essential for the health benefits of all, and the moral welfare of their workers. 'Hammersmith may well be proud of this park, which affords pleasure and recreation to classes and masses alike,' Sexby said in 1907.

It plays the same role today, offering a lake, tennis courts, nature area, bowling green, playground, a dog-free area and all-weather football pitches. The effect is rather controlled: lots of small areas boxed off for specific purposes, beds fenced with low hoops. The south side, where our tree sits, is a little more open and relaxed, and all around the park there's a fantastic collection of mature specimen trees, thanks to the Victorians. Sexby also noted that 'merry making is one of the objects for which Ravenscourt Park exists.' And that still sounds like a good idea.

GETTING THERE

Map ⑬

Location South end of Ravenscourt Park, W6. The nearest entrance is on Ravenscourt Road.
Access The park gates are open from dawn to dusk.
Transport Ravenscourt Park tube/ 27, 190, 266, 267, 391 bus.
Directions From the station turn right on to Ravenscourt Road, then left after the bridge into the park via the footpath. Walk around the tennis courts. The tree is to the left, halfway down the path going through the central open area.

The Ravenscourt Park Tree of Heaven

Ailanthus altissima

The name promises so much! The reality delivers… so much less than that. This *Ailanthus* is classified as an invasive weed in parts of the US and Australia, and there are concerns that it will become more problematic in Europe over the next few years, as the climate becomes more accommodating. To appreciate the tree, you need to look past such an inauspicious beginning, and beyond the expectation set up by its name. Maybe a story will help.

We open in China in the 1740s, where this tree has a long history, and where it was revered for its medicinal properties. Pierre Nicholas d'Incarville, a French botanist and Jesuit missionary tasked with converting the emperor, was sending seeds back to a Parisian botanist friend, Bernard de Jussieu. Jussieu sent some on to Philip Miller at the Chelsea Physic Garden, and to Philip C Webb, the owner of an exotic plant garden in Surrey. Each of the three men identified the tree with a different name, a confusion that got resolved 40 years later, when another French botanist observed the tree's little papery samara (keys, or fruits) and decided it was in the same genus as another tropical example, *Ailanthus tryphsa*. So, a rather romantic start; but when you get close to the tree, things go decidedly downhill.

For a start, the tree smells. It's been described as smelling like rotting peanut butter, and one of its common names in the US is stinking sumac. It's dioecious (each tree is either male or female) and the male flowers smell worse than the female. It suckers prodigiously, from its stem and shallow roots, crowding out all other plants. In a process called allelopathy, it also produces a toxic chemical that suppresses the germination and growth of other species nearby. The roots are damagingly aggressive and extensive, and it can quickly colonise derelict areas; it's called the ghetto palm in New York, and it's possible to date when a patch of land was abandoned by using the tree's height as a guide. It's an attractive ornamental, however: it grows quickly, and is very tolerant of pollution, aridity and rubbish soil. It's short-lived, but it's a good example of making the most of what you have.

Our tree stands in front of a low wall in a fenced-off part of Ravenscourt Park, one of a line of large trees along the edge that look like they're standing around waiting to be asked to dance. *Ailanthus* means 'reach for the sky', and *altissima* means 'tallest' – and this one is indeed tall and upright, with undulating branches and a good rounded crown. The dark trunk has a central main fissure, and cream-coloured, wrinkle-like surface fissures. Its height means that to really enjoy the foliage, it's best viewed from afar. This is a landmark tree, one of the largest specimens in Britain – though set to be one of the most unwelcome.

GETTING THERE

Map ⑭

Location South end of Ravenscourt Park, entrance on Ravenscourt Road, Hammersmith, W6.

Access The park gates are open from dawn to dusk.

Transport Ravenscourt Park tube/ 27, 190, 266, 267, 391 bus.

Directions From the station turn right on to Ravenscourt Road, then left after the bridge into the park via the footpath. Walk around the tennis courts. The tree is in the fenced-off area just past the children's playground, next to the green part of the wall on the right.

TREE OF HEAVEN
(AILANTHUS ALTISSIMA)
ONE OF THE LARGEST SPECIMENS
IN THE COUNTRY AND
ONE OF THE
GREAT TREES OF LONDON

LONDON TREE FORUM WWW.FORESTRY.GOV.UK

THIS PLAQUE IS SUPPORTED BY ESSO UK PLC
FOR TREES OF TIME AND PLACE

The Barn Elms Plane

Platanus x hispanica

'Barn Elms is a grand old estate, a few miles outside of London… What with its well-kept lawns, fine old trees, glimpses here and there of the Thames winding round its borders, and its wealth of old associations, it is, indeed, a charming spot,' wrote the American social activist Elizabeth Cady Stanton in 1898. It would be easy to conclude from this that everything was nicer in the olden days (as long as you were the one invited to the grand estate, not peeling the vegetables therein) – because there's no doubt that Barn Elms did sound nice.

It was – and in a more open way, still is. Then a country estate, meeting place of the elite, it's now a well-used green space on the south bank of the Thames, where the river goes into a tight loop, between Barnes and Putney. The landscape is as historic as the tree, with many famous residents and visitors – including Samuel Pepys, who 'took barge to visit friends by the sequestered and rural hamlet of Putney', as William Sharp wrote in *Literary Geography* in 1904. Pepys described the trip as 'mighty pleasant, the supping here under the trees by the waterside' – and at a guess, the supping was not lemonade, as they sang on the barge all the way home. Barn Elms Mansion (which burned down in the 1950s) was home to the Kit Cat Club, a meeting place for liberal politicians and literary talk, but mostly known for drinking toasts to the beautiful women of the day. The renowned Ranelagh Polo Club met there until the 1930s; the polo pitches became 'Dig For Victory' allotments in World War II.

Larger plane trees are often situated beside water, as they do best there. This tree is in a wooded ring around the anglers' pond, fenced off from the muddy field you stand in for viewing. Estimated to be one of the oldest planes in London, it was planted in the late 17th century, when planes were not such ubiquitous trees. It is still healthy, though it looks like an old man past his prime – he remembers his statuesque form, but finds it harder to maintain the pose. Everything is not quite as perfect as it probably once was; the bark, which flakes in plates on a younger tree, has become more persistent with age, and is now thick and cracked. The base is messy with thin new shoots, creeping ivy and a bird box. The tree sits behind a low fence, so, sadly, you can't even pat the old man.

When you're done contemplating the tree, head to the WWT London Wetland Centre next door. It was a fantastic addition to the city's urban escapes when it opened in 2000, becoming a Site of Special Scientific Interest (SSSI) within two years – a testament to the conservation work they do here with birds and other wetland wildlife.

GETTING THERE

Map ⑮

Location Barn Elms Park, Queen Elizabeth Walk, Barnes, SW13 9SA.
Access The park is open from dawn to dusk.
Transport Barnes rail/33, 72, 209, 283, 419, 485 bus.
Directions From Barnes station, follow signs to the Wetland Centre via Rocks Lane. At the crossroads with Church Street, turn right on to Queen Elizabeth Walk. Walk past the entrance to the Wetland Centre and take the gate on the right. With the tennis courts on your right, the plane is 20 yards ahead, to the right of the angling lake.

The Black Horse Pollard Chestnut

Aesculus hippocastanum

Some trees, like some people, are hard to love. That is true for this tree. But make the effort with this hard-to-love chestnut and – although it will still be a strange, dark sight – it will give back, at least in the ways of arboricultural education.

The horse chestnut, or conker tree, can reach around 260 feet – and a hit by a conker falling from such a height would really hurt. That possibility is obviated in this case: the tree is behind a waist-high wall, and when you spot the tree, you notice that the crown is only slightly higher than the wall. On first sighting, however, the difference between your knowledge and expectation of how a tree grows, and the reality of how this one *is* growing, plays a trick on your sense of perspective. So, your eyes tell your brain that there must be a steep drop just behind the wall, to accommodate the tree's long trunk. You walk up to the wall, and peer over, gripping on in careful readiness for the vertigo-inducing drop you're convinced is there. But there is no drop, because there is no long trunk. Instead it's short and stumpy, about two or three feet in length, atop of which is a twisted mass of thick, dark lumpen branches, all knobbled and bulging. Hundreds of thin whips spring upwards from the swollen ends of branches; everything the tree has to offer is within easy reach. Pollarding is a method to maintain a tree's vigour and potentially extend its lifespan – and there is no doubting that this tree has been heavily pollarded, being full of healed rounds where major cutting has taken place. What is less clear is why the trunk has remained so stunted, because not all pollarded trees are shorties.

As usual with our Great Trees, this stunted, twisted tree might squat square and ugly in its site, Rumplestiltskin-style, but it does have something special to offer, right at its heart. It's visible from the corner of a busy road junction, standing in a measly grassy area that used to be the back garden of a pub, the Black Horse, which was 'developed' into flats. Crane over and you can see an almost-perfect bowl created at the top of the central trunk by the curtailed branches, twisting round back on themselves. You'd have to wriggle, but once you were in there, it would have been a fantastic spot just for lying low, lounging in the leaves on a long Sunday. So, in cutting the higher branches to keep the growth low, the keepers of this tree have given us the tantalising glimpse of a secret hidey-hole. If only this was still a pub, we could all rendezvous there.

GETTING THERE

Map ⓰
Location 181 Sheen Road, East Sheen, TW9 1XF.
Access On private land, but visible over a low wall.
Transport North Sheen rail/ 190, 391, 419 bus.
Directions Turn left out of the station, then left again on to Manor Road, then down to the crossroads. Cross over Sheen Road, from where the tree is visible from behind a low wall.

LONDON TREE FORUM WWW.FORESTRY.GOV.UK

THE BLACK HORSE
POLLARDED CHESTNUT,
OF UNUSUAL SHAPE,
ONE OF THE
GREAT TREES OF LONDON

AESCULUS HIPPOCASTANUM

THIS PLAQUE IS SUPPORTED BY ESSO UK PLC
FOR TREES OF TIME AND PLACE

The Black Horse Pollard Chestnut

The Asgill House Copper Beech

Fagus sylvatica 'Purpurea'

If you're playing Fantasy Property Buying, Asgill House might just fit the bill for your south-west London residence; somewhere to retreat to in summer on the days when town gets a little clammy and you need a river breeze to cool off. You're a bit spoiled for choice in Richmond, so if you're going to buy here, the place has to go that extra mile. Asgill House, built in 1760 on the site of the Richmond Palace brewhouse, offers quite a few extra miles of history. In addition to being a grand old house with unusual octagonal rooms, there's a fantastic view, and nearby are some bijou local dining spots. Would a Great Tree in your garden clinch the deal? Because here, you get your hands on your own personal Great Tree – everyone else can look, but you can touch.

Asgill House, named after the banker it was built for, Sir Charles Asgill, is a gorgeous Palladian villa in golden stone, set back behind a semi-circular wall that separates its garden from the Thames towpath. It was the first major project of Sir Robert Taylor, one of the most prolific architects of his time (late 18th century), and it's still privately owned. Beside it, almost dwarfing it, is this beech tree, a magnificent specimen. The plaque on the garden wall describes it as a 'perfect tree', and indeed it is. It was planted in the early 1800s to celebrate the birth of a grandson, which is some expectation for that grandson to live up to. At around 200 years old, it has a glorious thick trunk and many branches emanating on all sides, like nature playing a huge game of Ker-plunk. The branches create a pristine round-headed crown, and produce a dense foliage – not much can grow under a beech tree. The tree dominates the view far more than the house does; and as you can only look at it through railings set in the semi-circular wall, that is a good thing.

Fagus sylvatica 'Purpurea' has a common name – the copper beech. It's a native tree that can be used for hedging, although it's hard to reconcile this specimen with that function. The bark is smooth, the leaves are dark purple in summer, making it even more noticeable against the surrounding greenery and the sky. They turn a bright burnished copper in autumn before dropping: the perfect complement to the gold of the stone building it sits beside. There are several ways you might encounter the tree. The towpath beside the Thames is a lovely walking route, or you might glimpse it from the train across the railway bridge right next door. Looking at the perfectly preserved buildings of the conservation area around you, it's easy to picture royal flotillas and merchant boats parading up and down the unspoiled river location, the tree sharing itself generously with the unobtrusive peace of ducks, walkers and river travellers.

GETTING THERE

Map ⑰

Location Asgill House, Old Palace Lane, Richmond, TW9 1PQ.
Access On private land, visible over a brick wall.
Transport Richmond tube/rail/65, 190, 371, 391, 419, 490 bus.
Directions From Richmond station, turn left down The Quadrant, then right into Duke Street, which leads to Richmond Green, on Old Palace Lane. Asgill House is at the far north-west corner of the Green, a 15-minute walk from the station.

The Maids of Honour Stone Pine

Pinus pinea

Richmond Green is very, very old – jousting tournament old. Cricket has been played here for ever, way before the earliest recorded fixture in 1730 (Surrey vs Middlesex; and for those who care about such things, Surrey won).

It's also very, very historic, its 400-year history – from the time when it first had houses built around it, for people working in or visiting nearby Richmond Palace – palpable. When you land here, even though there might be traffic bustle, the air has an other-worldly quality, a pervading sense of respect for things past, the kind of place that makes you keep your voice down. Architectural historian Nikolaus Pesvner described it as 'one of the most beautiful urban greens surviving anywhere in England.' It's lovely in its simplicity: a flat open square of grass crossed by centuries-old paths, framed by trees in front of some very fancy houses.

Head for the south-west side of the green. Some fine magnolias stand in front of Maids of Honour Row, a Georgian terrace of three-storey houses dating from 1724, used as lodging for the maids attending to the Princess of Wales. The handsome building beside them is the Gate House, one of the last remaining pieces of the Tudor-built Richmond Palace. From inside the turreted curve of the garden wall, pushing out and up, comes this exceptionally mature tree, standing solitary with dramatic aplomb. From a distance, it looks like a tall, thin giant with mad hair. It's in stark contrast to the other trees on the green; predominately limes, plus ubiquitous planes and recently added Norwegian maples. Early maps show that there would have been no planting at all on this side of the Green in Tudor times, giving ladies a better view of all the jousting action.

This is the only stone pine to make Great Tree status – they're a native of southern Europe, and rare in London (and not exactly common anywhere in Britain). There is a landmark one in Kew Gardens, aged around 150, but it's multi-branched, so not as 'textbook' as this specimen. This tree sits in a private garden, so our view is outside looking in, but as all you lose are the bottom eight feet of foliage-covered trunk, it doesn't feel like deprivation. The beautiful, long orange-brown trunk has an almost architectural quality, deeply grooved and fissured into vertical plates that look like glued-on lumps of papier mâché. There is one escaping lower branch that reaches across, overhanging the entrance road to the old wardrobe area of the Palace. The rest of the tree forges on up to create the upside-down foliage that befits its other name – umbrella pine. The thin, twisting paired needle leaves provide a good display for the heavy cones. In the Mediterranean, stone pines have been harvested for centuries, for pine nuts, an essential ingredient of classic Italian pesto.

GETTING THERE

Map ⑱

Location The Green, Richmond, TW9 1QQ.

Access On private land, visible over a brick wall.

Transport Richmond tube/rail/ 65, 190, 371, 391, 419, 490 bus.

Directions A 15-minute walk from the station. Exit left, then right into Duke Street and follow the road until it reaches the Green. The stone pine is at the south-western edge of the Green, behind a brick wall and next to a small lane called the Wardrobe.

The Maids of Honour Stone Pine

Within an acorn's throw...

Plan your visits to cover two or more trees in one outing.

It can be glaringly obvious when trees featured in this book are close together – the two with Ravenscourt in their title are both in Ravenscourt Park, for instance; and there are also two in Greenwich Park. Central London doesn't need too much extra billing, because it's easy to wander about in, and more familiar. Here are some suggestions for multi-tree visits elsewhere:

● The York House Cut Leaf Beech (*see p80*) and the Marble Hill Black Walnut (*see p76*) are within walking distance of each other. And it's also possible to tie in a visit to these with three more trees grouped together in Richmond – the Maids of Honour Stone Pine (*see p68*), the Asgill House Copper Beech (*see p66*) and the Riverside Plane (*see p72*).

● There are three trees in the Carshalton area: the Carshalton Plane (*see p192*), the Carshalton

Sweet Chestnut (*see p188*) and the Ashcombe Sweet Chestnut (*see p184*). If you go all the way to Downe to view its Yew, you may as well go the extra mile to see the Aperfield Cedar (*p210*), up the road.

● The Addington Palace Cedar of Lebanon (*see p206*) is a strenuous walk from the West Wickham Oak (*see p202*).

● It's possible to walk from Brixton (for the Tate Plane; *see p152*) up to Brockwell Park (for the Brockwell Oak; *see p154*).

● The Abbey Plane near Westminster Abbey (*see p28; below right*) is within walking distance of the Embankment Plane (*see p30; below left*).

● The Fairlop Oak (*see p120*) and the Valentine Maple (*see p116*) are in the same vicinity – quite a walk though, and not necessarily pleasant.

LONDON TREE FORUM WWW.FORESTRY.GOV.UK

THE RICHMOND
RIVERSIDE PLANE,
IS THE TALLEST OF ITS KIND
IN THE CAPITAL, AND IS A
GREAT TREE OF LONDON

PLATANUS X HISPANICA

THIS PLAQUE IS SUPPORTED BY ESSO UK PLC
FOR TREES OF TIME AND PLACE

The Riverside Plane

Platanus x hispanica

It's well known that planes make up half of London's trees, and it might feel like a task too far to get excited about another. But this particular plane won't feel over-familiar, because it's a behemoth – the kind of tree that makes you giddy to look straight up the trunk into the heart of it – in a gorgeous setting. As the name suggests, this one sits right beside the Thames, and as moist river valleys are the optimum growing environment for London planes, it's perhaps unsurprising that this is noted as the largest specimen in the capital.

The plane stands beside the Thames in Richmond (just beyond Richmond Bridge towards Petersham) and the beauty of the area definitely lends a gloss to the tree. The wide and varied walkway is lined with some huge old trees, and looking across the water they are a defining landscape feature. Along the Thames Path, in two strides you can go from the quaint to the majestic, from buildings old and rickety to things of grandiose proportion. This plane is in the latter camp. It sits, or rather, powers from the ground, in a small restaurant dining deck – lit up, meagrely fenced off and surrounded by horrid white gravel. All that peripheral detail is rendered temporary by the robust sense of permanence of the tree itself. Even the ivy climbing it has given up after 20 feet. The trunk is solid and exudes vigour. It has casually chucked out a couple of lower branches, then forged on, thick-waisted as far as the eye can see. The crown is taller than it is broad, and you get the feeling that this tree could just keep going on and on. There is no reason, at this stage, to doubt that; we haven't yet discovered the end of the London plane's lifespan – the oldest specimens in Britain have lasted for more than 300 years, and are still in vigorous growth.

Be careful stepping back to get a real eyeful of this tree: you might get wet. To obtain a different view, you can hop over (not literally) to the footpath on the other side of the river. This gives a view of what it means for a tree to be head and shoulders above its fellows. Because of its location, it really is worth picking the right day to see it. A beautiful spring or autumn day brings out the best of the waterside. The tree has an attractive yellow-gold colour in autumn, and planes keeps their leaves longer than most, into early winter. If it's not asking too much, try to time it for a blue-sky day, maybe an unusually warm one. Then a meander along the river, keeping pace with a duck or two, and stopping at a nearby bench or outdoor café, is an unseasonal and highly recommended treat.

GETTING THERE

Map ⑲

Location Next to Gaucho Grill restaurant, The Towpath, Richmond, TW10 6UJ.
Access The river footpath is public land.
Transport Richmond tube/rail/ 65, 190, 371, 391, 419, 49 bus.
Directions Turn left out of Richmond station, and head along the Quadrant and then George Street. After you've passed House of Fraser on the right-hand side, veer left around the corner and then head down Water Lane, which leads to the river towpath. Turn left down the towpath; the tree is after Richmond Bridge.

The Marble Hill Black Walnut

Juglans nigra

In the 1720s Henrietta Howard was financially rewarded for her position as mistress to King George II, and put her money into property. The house that Henrietta built was the Marble Hill, a gorgeous Palladian villa elegantly set in acres of parkland that gently roll down to the Thames. Now an English Heritage site, it was intended as a pastoral retreat from the crowded streets of London in the hottest months, and the lively and intelligent Mrs Howard held famed summer salons here, for the great wits of her day.

Among those gathered in her drawing room was poet Alexander 'Rape of the Lock' Pope, credited in the planning of the garden – it may have been he who chose the black walnut tree down near the river, giving us probably the oldest and certainly the largest specimen in the country. The tree stayed up in the storm of 1987 when many others in the park did not; that, and the protective fence around it, give it a sense of being a survivor. It's hanging on in there – literally, in the case of the main branch leading away from the river, now held in place by tension wires. But the careful management of the tree, with obvious evidence of limb removal, suggests it will survive, even if its glory days are behind it. The encircling fence, light and token, is wider than the full extent of the longest limb, a clear message that if this tree sent down a branch, you would know about it. Keeping a wide berth means you have to view from a small distance away, but actually, it's almost best admired from right across the field. Enjoy the moment when you first spot it in all its blackness, and immediately know 'ah, that's the one'.

This tree is beautifully distinctive from every direction. It's not the most symmetrical tree or of the most pleasing shape or stunning size. It's at its most flamboyant during spring-into-summer, in full green, with compound, odd-numbered pinnate leaves and bright bobbly-round fruit – walnuts, of course. But in winter it is, undoubtedly, stark and glorious. The compelling black bark creates a border separating it from everything around, like the sharp and dense colour of a felt-tip pen outlining a muted swathe of blue and green crayon.

Black walnuts aren't native to this country. They're primarily found in eastern North America, imported here in the early 17th century for the renowned quality of their wood. The hulls of black walnuts produce an indelible ink used in the past as a dye, and while the English walnut is easier to crack, it's not as fully flavoured and therefore not such a prize. Where Nature gives with one hand, she takes with the other: all parts of the black walnut tree secrete a chemical called juglone, which, when combined with air or soil, produces an effect called allelopathy – toxicity to other trees and plants that might have dared to grow beneath or around the tree. Good judgement (or maybe allelopathy), means this tree stands alone, so can't wreak its havoc on other planting.

GETTING THERE

Map 20

Location Marble Hill Park, Richmond Road, Twickenham, TW1 2NL.
Access The park is open from dawn to dusk.
Transport St Margarets rail/33, 490, H22, H37, R68, R70 bus.
Directions Turn right out of the station, then fork right down Crown Road. Cross over Richmond Road into Orleans Road and head down to the Thames. Go left along the river footpath until you reach the entrance to Marble Hill Park. The black walnut is 20 yards ahead, to the right.

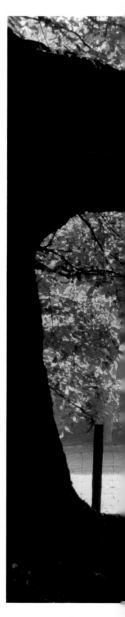

The York House Cut Leaf Beech

Fagus sylvatica 'Asplenifolium'

If you like a bit of intentional mutation – and who doesn't? – this is an interesting example. Like the oak and sycamore, most of us could probably draw a beech leaf just from the memory of the school nature table. But the cut leaf beech is not quite that: it's a chimaera, a complex-sounding botanical cultivation where the inner tissues of an ordinary beech are overlaid by the tissues of the cut leaf form. It's sometimes called a 'sport', which gives it a robust jolly-hockey sound, but actually this can be a fragile state of existence, producing leaves of a much finer, more fingered, almost willowish appearance; damage to the tree can cause leaves to revert to their common type. The cultivar was developed in Europe in the 1820s as an ornamental, which fits well with the dating of this tree's surroundings. The tree is a well-managed specimen, with a strong crown, satisfyingly even in shape. The branches, like lean sinewed arms resting on one other, are close-growing and crossing; the smooth grey bark is displayed on a short trunk. Ten minutes on the bench beneath the tree, overlooking the river, is time well spent.

The beech sits in the grounds of York House, once a private mansion, now the town hall for the borough of Richmond upon Thames. There are lots of York Houses around, all so-called because they were residences for the Duke of York. This one is different – the names comes from the Yorke family, who farmed the area in the 17th century, when the house was built. It's a rather lovely building, used for marriages and the like, but the Palladian splendour is definitely tempered by council signage. The front garden is now mostly a car park, the back gardens are posh-municipal, with neat paths and play-safe planting. The path down to the river leads over a stone bridge, across a tarmac road that divides the main garden from the river terrace. Up another set of steps, and the first sight across the river, on Eel Pie Island, is a large working boatyard – a blunt reminder of the reality outside.

Not that all the classic garden architecture is tasteful, however. There is one memorable element that takes the phrase 'over the top' to another level altogether. Ostentatious, fabulously camp, a bit of folly: a collection of statues, built on a large scale in Italian white marble. They depict the Oceanides, sea nymphs from Greek mythology, not usually known for their connections with downtown Richmond. These nymphs, draped for modesty in sparse bits of cloth, sprawl up various rocky, watery cascades and crawl through green ponds and out of oversized shells, with stone expressions ranging from bored to medicated. They reach towards two rearing winged horses who guard a standing nymph. No analysis required. Is it sacrilege to say it's worth the trip just to see this alone?

GETTING THERE

Map ㉑

Location Next to the Thames, behind York House, Richmond Road, Twickenham, TW1 3AA.
Access The grounds of York House are open dawn to dusk.
Transport Twickenham rail/ 33, 490, H22 bus.
Directions Turn left out of the station, then left at the T-junction with York Street. York House is 50 yards ahead on the right. Enter by the main entrance, and follow the left-hand path round to the back of the house and the far end of the garden. Cross the footbridge, and once at the river, the beech is just to the left.

The Richmond Royal Oak

Quercus robur

Here in Richmond Park, you stare at millions of trees, thinking you're looking for a needle in a massive haystack, but once you get towards the right area, it's true enough – in the land of giants, our short fat tree is visible from right across the view.

Richmond Park is sublime, exceptional, unique. Every which way there are things of glory. You are totally spoiled for choice for fantastic trees, birds, animals, beetles, views, lakes, benches and cycling outfits. With a perfect sky, it's a holiday. The trees of Richmond are amazing; all of them. Every blade of grass is a marvel, every polite plip of deer poo. There is too much history to précis in such a short space, and too much marvellous stuff to mention. If you visit just *one* tree in this book, visit this one. Although the secret is most definitely out…

If you end up walking across Richmond Park from its Kingston side, you get your first view of the tree right in the distance across two lakes, known as Pen Ponds. Something in the distance draws your eye. Something differently green. As you approach, across rolling grassland maintained just this side of glorious, there's a short fat tree encircled by much taller ones, but with a wide space cleared around it – like that created as school bullies back off from the small angry kid with karate skills. As you get near, you can't believe you could have spotted the right tree from so far away. It's clearly a magic tree! It makes you see it, where ordinarily you would not. And what a perfectly magic tree it is. Short, yes, because of centuries-old pollarding; and gnarled and holey with the sun shining in; and lumpen and with a split right down the centre, leaving just enough of a crack for children to push themselves in for photos – a great place to find a secret message in a historical drama. The wood is different every way you look; some dark and twisted, other parts almost cork-coloured, with swirling textured lumps. Not every short character is good for comedy; this one is a little ominous, with its arms extended, as if to poke you suddenly with a bony old finger. At angles it becomes hunched and brooding, but then it's had a long time to brood – it's estimated to be around 750 years old (though you can't count the rings of a hollow trunk). It's definitely medieval, and though the Lycra count will be higher now than then, the immediate landscape won't have changed dramatically.

There is a perfectly placed bench right beside the tree, with a superb view. On it you can contemplate the hundreds of other veteran oak trees in Richmond Park. But such is its magic, this one will likely remain your favourite.

GETTING THERE

Map ㉒

Location North-west corner of Richmond Park. The nearest entrance is Richmond Gate, TW10.
Access The park is open from 7am in summer (7.30am winter) and closes at dusk.
Transport Richmond tube/rail then 65, 371 bus/33, 337, 485 bus.
Directions From the roundabout at Richmond Gate, follow Sawyer's Hill, and then take the footpath that runs along the north-eastern side of Sidmouth Wood. Follow the path around the wood's eastern side, near Queen Elizabeth's Plantation, to the north-west of Pen Ponds. Here you'll find the oak.

The Roehampton Lucombe Oak

Quercus x hispanica 'Lucombeana'

The story of this tree starts with two men of the mid 18th century, which, given the immediate surroundings, will stretch even the most active imagination. The first man is William Lucombe, an Exeter nursery man who, in 1762, noticed seedlings that crossed the turkey oak with the cork oak. In the wild, this is a naturally occurring hybrid, but he propagated it and gave it his name. The second man, at around the same time, is one of the founding fathers of landscape design, Capability Brown – real name Lancelot. Capability, who died in 1783, described himself as a 'place-maker' rather than a gardener. He designed many huge estates and parks throughout England, with west London's Syon Park a good example of his work. He had a consultancy role in landscaping the gardens of Grove House (on Roehampton Lane, and now part of Roehampton University) just up the road from this tree, and it's in this building's former grounds that we now stand – in a grey 1950s housing estate, envisaging the tree as part of a one-time grand garden scheme.

The story now leaps forward to the near-present. The Alton Estate is right on the edge of Richmond Park, Roehampton Golf Course and Putney Heath: green spaces that have come to symbolise old rock-star and new hedge-fund wealth. They are packed with the sort of grand Grade-I and -II listed buildings we have come to understand as 'heritage'. On the Alton Estate, meanwhile, there's a different kind of heritage, not universally seen as classic, but certainly as relevant – perhaps more so by dint of the number of people it concerns. This heritage is rooted in the post-World War II period, when new homes for 'the masses' were a priority. And where some might see tower blocks on a housing scheme, others see an architectural battle raging between this part of the estate (Alton West) and another, just minutes to the south (Alton East). Between the pure Modernist architecture of Le Corbusier that triumphed at Alton West – the closest thing Britain has to his vision of L'unité d'habitation in Marseille – and the Swedish Modernism at Alton East. Understanding their provenance helps you to look at these places with a little more generosity.

In this story of big important men, our tree definitely becomes a minor player, even though it's said to be the largest of its species in London. Individual Lucombe oaks vary considerably: on some the bark is thick and corky; on some it's thin; on others the more normal blackish. This one has grey corrugated bark; it's semi-deciduous, with leaves that resemble traditional oak leaves but stretched out, so the lobes become pointed. It's a tall and slender column, reaching nearly as high as the block beside it. It has reached full height, but would have to really pull something out of the bag to dominate this landscape and take a more dramatic role in the story.

GETTING THERE

Map ㉓

Location Alton Estate, Roehampton, SW15.

Access On public land and accessible at all times.

Transport Barnes rail/72, 85, 170, 265, 430, 493 bus.

Directions A 25-minute walk from Barnes station. Turn right, then right again on to Rocks Lane. At the crossroads with the Upper Richmond Road, go straight ahead into Roehampton Lane. Continue, past Roehampton University, until you reach Danebury Avenue. Turn right; the oak is in front of the third housing block on the right.

The Osterley Park Cork Oak

Quercus suber

Corky doesn't even come close. The bark more resembles thick honeycomb dripping like clinging rivers down the trunk. Convoluted, riven, gouged, thick enough to create shadows within itself. The texture of abandoned wasps' nests or ancient sea stone, so detailed it looks as if things might have fossilised in it.

Who would have thought? Well, the residents round the edge of Osterley Park would have, but if you're not one of those, this is a very pleasant surprise. It's a surprise in the sense that the environs don't give much away. The park is split in two by the dispiriting M4, with its southern edge running alongside the equally dispiriting A4. But one minute away from a congested main road, and you come across a stately avenue of massive chestnut trees, fields of horses and even a farm shop. Only the landing carriage of a 747 perilously close to your head will remind you that Heathrow is just up the road.

Osterley Park has an eponymous mansion attached, a neo-classical villa that gained a reputation in the 1880s as an all-weekender party house. It's now in the hands of the National Trust, so the kind of parties it hosts today have sensible shoes and like a bit of proper ice-cream. The cork oak sits beside a lake with a back view of the big house; it's a fantastic location, perfect for a wander, and the size and scope of some of the nearby cedars on the lawn will undoubtedly dazzle your eye. This tree does not have their height or immediacy, but it has a trunk and shape that is very distinctive. It's a fabulous specimen, totally relaxed in its aged splendour; the short main bole divides into great rough branches, which lean away from the lake and touch the ground in places, a common trait of these trees as they age. Some 250 years in, it's vigorous in leaf and seed, with masses of leaves hanging almost vertically, so the tree gives an atmospheric dry rustle in a breeze, which you can appreciate from the shady bench beneath.

Cork oaks are native to the western Mediterranean and thrive in hot, arid conditions completely unlike those presented by west London. Portuguese and Spanish cork oak forests are ancient, and thus host to fantastic ecosystems; the World Wildlife Fund describes them as 'top biodiversity hotspots'. The cork oak forests are a great example of a traditional sustainable industry – for as long as people need cork. When the cork is harvested, the brighter inner bark of the tree is exposed. Newly bare, it is as odd a sight as a decorative dog's quaking pink skin when freshly shorn. Cork is a renewable resource, so the trees grow a new coat over the next ten years. But when they've been grown as ornamentals – as in this case – the cork is left undisturbed, which accounts for its extruded artistry, a superb piece of living sculpture.

GETTING THERE

Map ㉔

Location Osterley Park, Jersey Road, Isleworth, Hounslow, TW7 4RB.
Access The park is open from 8am to 7.30pm (6pm Nov-Mar).
Transport Osterley tube/ H28, H91 bus.
Directions Turn left out of the station along the Great West Road, then left into Thornbury Road. This leads straight into the park. Follow the path around the lake, keeping to the right; the cork oak is just past the house. It's a 20-minute walk in all.

GREAT TREES OF LONDON

The Osterley Cork Oak
Quercus suber
Awarded 18 November 2008
by Trees for Cities
www.treesforcities.org

Sponsored by Barratt Homes and Magic 105.4

East

The Stratford Fig

Ficus carica

Not all people find beauty in the same things. Not all of us define 'great' in the same way. In a cityscape, there can be poetry in the shapes two cranes form high in the air; there can be drama in the way buildings reveal themselves as they are built; and there can be pleasure in finding something green amongst all the grey.

This fig makes it on to the Great Tree list for very individual reasons, none of them about traditional aesthetics. It's not pretty. The land was never part of a historic great estate, and if it ever was a hunting ground, pitbulls would have been involved. It makes the list because it displays a gritty determination to survive and thrive in the most un-natural place. The trunk starts beside what is loosely called a river, though it's the kind of water that redefines the word – it is liquid, but barely, and it makes your skin come out in a rash just looking at it. The tree grows up the bank surrounded by pylons, metal spiked fences, an industrial bridge and thick pipes, all of which it cleverly uses as props for its branches.

It also makes the list because it symbolises the successful immigrant in the East End, of which there are many examples right through London's history. The East End has traditionally been a place where incoming communities settle and the tree is a fantastic green example of that – of something putting down roots in a hostile place. But determination and symbolism aside, to be a Great Tree, the tree must also have physical qualities, and this one hides the fact that it's a fantastic specimen. You come at it from above, and have to make an effort, scrambling round on the accessible sides to get a sense of where it really starts. The glorious invader is best appreciated up close, early in the year, when it has no leaves to mask the inner kerfuffle, so you can get a real sense of how it has colonised and adapted. From the main trunk, there are hundreds of large and small soft branches, growing up the sloping scrappy bank and across the bridge, creeping into every available space. It's full of shoots in the middle, very vigorous, erect, defiant almost. A wonderfully successful tree.

The fig is sited on Joseph Bazalgette's construction of the late 1850s, glamorously called the Northern Outfall Sewer. So there is history here, of a particular sort. Five miles of the sewer's route has been turned into a walkway, the Greenway, but it's really only for the most dedicated lover of grotty urban decay. It's also perilously close to all the Olympic construction for 2012. A building site offers a fairly bleak position for the tree – not an optimistic outlook. But in the end, being on a list might be the saviour of it: now the fig has been 'officially' recognised, it may, for the first time, receive a little care and attention.

GETTING THERE

Map ㉕
Location Greenway, by the footbridge over the Waterworks River, just off the High Street, Stratford, E15.
Access The footpath is accessible during daylight hours.
Transport Pudding Mill Lane DLR/ 25, 108, 276, 425, D8 bus.
Directions From the station, walk to the Greenway footpath via Pudding Mill Lane and Marshgate Lane, then continue east back under the railway bridge. The fig tree is another 150 yards ahead, by the footbridge on the right, just before the High Street. Note that the footpath is closed until spring 2010 for Olympic site construction; call 08000 722 110 for details, or visit www.jubileegreenway.com.

The Wood Street Horse Chestnut 🍃

Aesculus hippocastanum

Minor shopping streets specialising in cheap shoes and plastic storage boxes in the outer reaches of the city aren't much of a draw. But real London from the perspective of Great Trees also includes unprepossessing places.

This tree doesn't look grand, and the shop it sits outside doesn't, either. But that is real history – often not grand, and very accessible. This tree is certainly the latter, sitting just off the pavement behind a neat white picket fence in front of what looks like a painted-up shed. Actually, this low, white wooden building is a Grade II-listed example of an 18th-century weatherboard shop, the oldest such shop in the borough that has remained so. It's now a purveyor of organic goods, but for nearly 200 years it was Jones the Butcher. The business passed from father to son, and it came complete with its own slaughterhouse; some local people still remember sheep being herded down Wood Street to meet their end. What is now a car park to the rear of the shop was once grazing ground for these animals. It was called the Hoppit, obviously named by someone with a dark sense of humour. Envisaging that scene, with a soundtrack of final, tragic bleats, is hard over the traffic.

So to the tree, estimated to be 175 years old. Like a cork being pulled from a bottle, the trunk twists round until it reaches roof height, and then the branches fly out in all directions, forming a fine crown right across and above the shop. Horse chestnuts are very generous trees, changing their decorative features every season so they're always offering something new. In spring, their buds are shining sticky beads, glossy bits of jewellery glistening at the end of each twig. Around April/May, they produce masses of distinctive flowers – white, upright, conical panicles evoking candles, sitting on top of the flopping, multi-fingered leaf. Horse chestnuts are really at their stunning best at this time. It's when they produce their fruit, which starts off as a green, spiky ball. These split to release the ultimate symbol of an old-school childhood: the shiny brown chestnut we know as the conker. Horse chestnuts aren't actually native to this country; they were introduced from the Balkans in the early 1500s. However, they're so much a part of the scenery that they now feel like 'ours'. The game of conkers – drilling holes and threading the nuts on string, then whacking your opponent's conker as hard as you can – is thought to be around 200 years old, its name derived from 'conquerors'. Dipping your conkers in vinegar or baking them to make them harder is considered cheating, and would get you kicked out of the conker club. It's heritage in the form of a Health & Safety nightmare, and since 1965, has been elevated to international championship level, with a tournament held annually in Northamptonshire.

GETTING THERE

Map ㉖

Location Outside Second Nature shop, 78 Wood Street, Walthamstow, E17 3HX.
Access Just off a public road and accessible at all times.
Transport Wood Street rail/ 123, 275 bus.
Directions From platform 1 at the station, turn right, then right again into Wood Street and under the railway bridge. The horse chestnut is 150 yards ahead, on the left.

The chestnut: horse versus sweet

How to differentiate between the two.

Why are two very different trees from different families referred to under the same name? The two main kinds of chestnut, the horse chestnut (*Aesculus hippocastanum*) and the sweet chestnut (*Castinea sativa*) are not even distantly related, and neither are native to the UK. The leaves and blossom are completely different: horse chestnuts have five- or seven-palmate leaves (*below left*) and upright coned panicles of flowers; sweet chestnuts have oblong, toothed leaves (*below right*) and tiny flowers beneath the catkins. The only similarity is their fruit: both produce a small, round, brown nut, but even those are distinct – the sweet chestnut is a bit ridged and has a little point, and the horse chestnut conker is round and smooth. The sweet chestnut is the edible one, planted by the Romans as they made their way around Europe, when chestnuts were a major source of carbohydrate. Horse chestnuts are horrible, and poisonous. Best not get them confused.

The name sweet chestnut makes sense – it is sweet(ish), and it is a chestnut. So why horse chestnut? There is a variety of offerings, which do a nice job of muddying the water. Some suggest that *Aesculus* comes from *esca* (food) and others that it's from *aesculin* (poison), but that might be putting the cart before the horse, as the poison may be named after the tree and not the other way round. Some think that the horse prefix comes from the Welsh word *gwres*, or hot, bitter – to distinguish the foul-tasting chestnut from the sweet one. The word 'horse' can be used to mean strong. (Horse chestnuts have a reputation, and let it remain apocryphal, as being useful for horses with wind problems.) Or maybe it comes from the horseshoe-shaped mark left on the twig by the leaf when it drops. *Hippocastanum* is the Greek for horse (*hippo*) followed by the Latin for sweet chestnut. Confused? Botanical names are supposed to clarify things; this one does a great job in making things less clear.

Add this to the mix: there is also a red version of the horse chestnut – *Aesculus x carnea*, a hybrid of the common horse chestnut and the *Aesculus pavia*. They sometimes make their way into an otherwise perfect avenue of horse chestnuts, much to the delight or disgust of tree experts, depending on your love of symmetry. It's similar in leaf to the common horse chestnut, but has show-off pinky-red flowers to distinguish it.

Finally, don't waste your time looking for the tree that produces the Chinese water chestnut. These are from the roots of an aquatic plant.

The North Circular Cork Oak 🍃

Quercus suber

This is not a book of arboreal advice, but here are two pieces anyway: first, don't judge a tree by your journey to it; and second, try not to judge a tree by the position it is in. There may be a little road beside this cork oak, cutely named Cork Tree Way; but don't be fooled! Your picnic is no good here.

Clinging on in a little corner with underpasses and overpasses and multi-laned roads and car parks and hangar-size superstores, there sits the cork oak. It is fenced in, the one little bit of old nature left in this modern car-opolis. Your first thought upon seeing the oak is that it doesn't seem well. You may well look at the amount of leaf loss littering the pavement and try to work out if you can dig the tree up and transplant it to a place where it might flourish more effectively. But the more you look, the more you realise that this is a gorgeous little tree. The trunk is thin, with the waspy texture of cork that resembles creamy toffee bubbling out, then cooling in weird formations. It's sweet. And it's still here, upright, going strong. Given the context, that's some achievement.

This tree isn't here by accident. The Cork Manufacturing Company had its factory just over the way, and although each cork oak can produce up to 4,000 corks per tree, this one was probably symbolically planted. Ads from the 1920s proudly talk about how the company has 'all grades of granulated cork', and 'sheet and strip cork for covering handles of all sports goods'. It's a good fit that the tree is around 100 years old. The leaves are simple, leathery and elliptical, dark green on top, fuzzy white underneath. Cork oaks, being in the oak genus, produce acorns! They do well in southern England. They do even better in the Med: Portugal's environmental laws have protected its cork forests since the 13th century, and in the 18th century, the monk Dom Pierre Pérignon was the first to use cork, allied with slender metal cages, to seal the bottles of his famous champagne. But the connection between cork and wine goes way back, to the fourth century BC; remains of cork bottle stoppers have been found in Egyptian tombs and at Pompeii. Pliny the Elder (AD 23-79), in his encyclopedia *Naturalis Historia*, detailed how cork oak trees symbolised liberty and honour to the ancient Greeks, and therefore only priests were allowed to cut them down. Dioscorides, a Greek doctor from the second century, recommended them for other purposes: 'charred cork rubbed on bald patches with laurel sap makes the hair grow again, thicker and darker than before,' he stated. Pictures of Dioscorides reveal a man who should probably have heeded his own advice.

GETTING THERE

Map ㉗

Location Hall Lane (behind the Chingford Audi dealership), Chingford, E4 8JA.

Access On a public road and accessible at all times.

Transport Highams Park rail/444 bus.

Directions It's a 35-minute walk from Highams Park station. Cross over James Yard and turn right into Larkshall Road. As it bends right, left off Larkshall Road into Ropers Avenue, then first right into Inks Green. Take this road straight over two crossroads, into Ainslie Wood Road, then Sinclair Road. The oak is at the end, by an elevated section of the North Circular, and surrounded by a blue fence.

The Friday Hill Plane

Platanus x hispanica

Once you know that this tree is opposite Pimp Hall Park, certain images might come to mind involving *Super Fly* types in wide-lapelled velvet suits, low gold Cadillacs cruising the area with blacked-out windows, and a large amount of bling.

It's not like that. It's about as far from that as is possible. The park is now a nature reserve, but dates back to Tudor times, when it was Pympe's Hall. It's most famous now for the historic dovecote it contains. Sorry if that disappoints.

The Friday Hill plane sits in the back garden of the eponymous house, just beyond the north-east corner, as you look at the building. The tree leans over the edge of a most inglorious car park, which is the viewing point. It sits in ground that's slightly higher than the car park level, so you come in almost under the tree; it hovers above you. This provides an improved perspective of the tree, early in the leafing season at least, as it moves from the bud phase. You look up through the twisting branches to the sky broken into millions of tiny pieces by each bit of emerging green. New leaves as they appear are bright and light; they don't give that heavy, dark cover of plane leaves yet, so the tree appears quite open and dainty, looking much more delicate at this point in the season than it will later. Pretty, almost – which is not a quality normally associated with planes. It's not an exceptional plane tree; but it is tall, probably dating from the building of the house, and long since dwarfing it. Low down on the trunk are knobs and sags, evidence of cut branches. One long branch curls and twists right across to the car park.

Friday Hill House was built as a manor house at the top of the world – or the top of Chingford, at least, which might in 1839 have seemed like the same thing. Designed by Lewis Vulliamy, it replaced a Tudor house, and was a home to the Boothby Heathcotes until 1940, when it went into council ownership on the death of the remaining family member. The original patriarch, RB Heathcote, was a rector and lord of the manor, and he must have been a good and wealthy sort as he built Chingford Infant School in 1856 (which is still open) and restored the parish almshouses. Both his house and school have blue plaques. RB is also noted as the owner of an oak table on which James I was said to have knighted a 'Sir' loin of beef, so fine was this particular bit of meat. However, the same table seems to appear in various other old manor houses round the country, which would suggest that the knighting of a cut of meat is an apocryphal tale.

GETTING THERE

Map ㉖

Location Grounds of Friday Hill House, Simmons Lane, Chingford, Essex E4 6JH.

Access The gates to the house are open from 9am to 9pm Monday to Thursday, 9am to 3pm Friday, and occasional Saturdays (call 8496 2980). The tree is also visible from the road.

Transport Chingford rail/212, 397 bus.

Directions A 30-minute walk from the station. Turn left on to Station Road, then left on to King's Road. Walk down King's Road, then turn right after the bridge into Friday Hill. At the crest of the hill, turn right into Simmons Lane. Friday Hill House is on the left. Turn right into the car park of the house; the plane is on the left.

The South Woodford Copper Beech

Fagus sylvatica 'purpurea'

Early spring, and without leaf, is an odd time to recommend a copper beech, but it's at this time that these trees push out their lovely buds – perfect metallic slivers that glint like fat pins in the sunshine. You also get to appreciate the naked structure of a tree at this time of year, and this one has masses of branches on all sides, a bit unsymmetrical but, hey, that's nature. In turn, up top it's awash with smaller erect branches, indicating how healthy it is. In full leaf it's a great purply stand, only becoming drily copper-coloured in winter. The crown is a splendid, almost perfect shape; very large, rearing over the church in whose front drive it sits. The trunk is a corded, thick grey-green, while the buttressed base is meagrely cordoned off and under-planted with a couple of spring bulbs that just serve to highlight their own loneliness. There are several old tombstones resting nearby, but the whole scene is a little barren. The gardens are not sumptuous, but have packed a lot in; it's called making the best of the situation.

The beech is in the front drive of St Mary's Church, and there are some impressive pieces of ancient statuary in dark garden corners. Be warned: Martha Pelly's memorial, behind and to the right of the church, might make you feel slightly inadequate. According to the huge neo-classical mausoleum she shares with husband William Raikes, she was someone 'in whom the conjugal, the parental, and all the relative virtues were heightened by the advantages of a superior understanding'. This was in MDCCXCVII, you understand (1797, if your Latin numerals fail you) – and don't linger too long on what a heightened conjugal virtue might be. Just pay your respects to a rather busy woman.

Other tombs offer useful hints on the area. In the front grassy bank lies buried William Morris Senior, father of William 'Arts and Crafts' Morris, alongside Emma, William Sr's wife. The Morris family lived for a while at Woodford Hall next door. The house is gone, and a parish hall now stands on the site, but the old boundary walls are still visible along the start of Chelmsford Road. The fact that William roamed freely as a youngster in nearby Epping Forest was said to have been a huge influence; when his father died, the family moved a couple of miles away to Water House in Walthamstow, which is now a dedicated Morris gallery.

The church itself, though it has artefacts dating from the 1550s, is the least interesting element of the site, partly because it has an architecturally dull flat frontage, an addition in 1969 after a fire. But at least there is a bench in front of the tree where you can hang your kagoul, open a flask and watch the traffic going at caravan speed on the old road out of London.

GETTING THERE

Map ㉙

Location Grounds of St Mary's Church, 207 High Road, South Woodford, E18 2PA.

Access The churchyard is accessible at all times.

Transport South Woodford tube/ 123, 179, W13 bus.

Directions Turn left out of the main station entrance, and head up the hill into George Lane. Go past the shops, with the green on your right. At the top of George Lane, turn right into the High Road and cross the North Circular; St Mary's is another 100 yards ahead, on the left. The beech is to the right as you walk through the church gates.

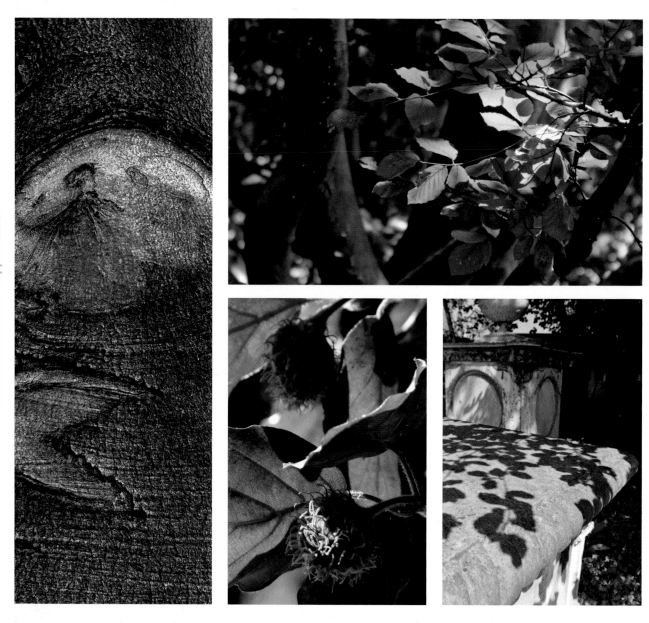

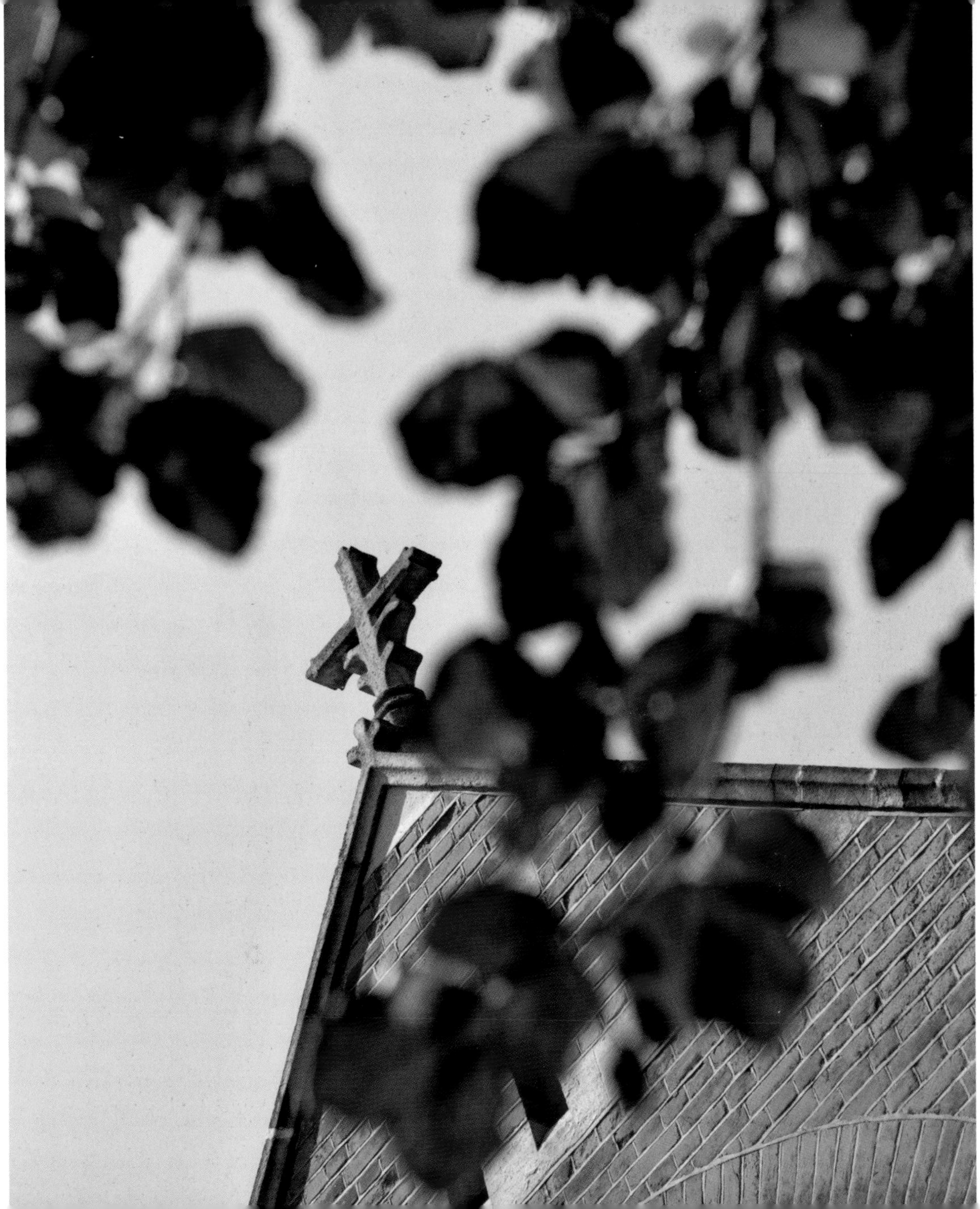

The George Green Sweet Chestnut

Castanea sativa

This is the story of a thin tranche of history, followed by a fat tranche of activism on George Green. It is one of three old sweet chestnuts in a lovely straight line: Daddy, Mummy and the sadly disfigured Baby, who got struck by lightning and lost half his trunk. Our tree is the Daddy, and has a great trunk, full of character. It's broad and gnarled, bulky and misshapen; from every angle you see bulging features like so many gouty noses. Old sweet chestnuts reek of history – they wear their heritage with the glorious pride of a Chelsea Pensioner. They're not tall, however: although members of the species have reached nearly 100 feet, these have gone out rather than up. The battering of the elements naturally keeps the crown relatively short. They are stocky and substantial reminders of weather past.

These specimens sit to one side of an urban common, the straight line a clue to their origins. Like other Great Trees, they were planted – probably in the early 1700s – on one of the mansion estates that made up outlying London, on part of an avenue leading from Wanstead House. These three trees went on to survive when another of their species on the green did not. It was a casualty of a landmark modern battle – that of cars and money versus people.

It had rumbled on for years, but in 1993 George Green finally became the loser in the face of petrol-driven progress: a new link road to the M11 got the go-ahead. The developers hadn't bargained on anti-road protesters, a potent combination of activists and local people, everyone from the oldest resident to a lollypop lady who galvanised children and parents – ordinary people who cared passionately about this green space, and in particular this trees. One of the sweet chestnuts became the centre of attention; people took up residence in it as a protest, and a way of safeguarding its existence. The tree got its 15 minutes: it got a mention in Hansard (the record of government debate) and the High Court recognised it as a legal dwelling, because the Royal Mail delivered post to a temporary letterbox up in its branches. It was the first time the country had really seen activism like it. But it did not end well: the only way to get people out of the tree was to cut it down. A symbolic death – the power of the chainsaw over the power of people. Parts of this tree still lie on the green rotting like a corpse on a battlefield long after the war is over.

GETTING THERE

Map

Location George Green, Cambridge Park, Wanstead, E11 2PU.
Access On public land that's accessible at all times.
Transport Wanstead tube/ 66, 101, 145, 308 bus.
Directions Leave Wanstead station by the left exit, walk up the steps and cross the road into George Green. Some 30 yards ahead to the left are a group of three sweet chestnuts. The Great Tree is the one with the widest trunk.

The Valentines Park Maple

Acer campestre

If ever a tree trunk embodied the Van Gogh style, this is it: a corky 'impasto' stream of bark meanders down the tree in short dynamic bursts, going round the carbuncle growths like water round stepping stones. It gives the trunk a sense of lazy movement, in the way that silt ridges on a dry riverbed show how things once passed by.

This is the only field maple to reach Great Tree status, and the only maple in a large family, including sycamores, that's native to Britain. Typical to maples, it has lobed palmate leaves, less precisely cut than some of its finer relations (the Japanese maples particularly) and great autumn colour, which gives it a role as an ornamental. The flowers are small and greeny-yellow, and in autumn, maples produce samara – papery two-winged helicopter fruits that twirl sweetly down. Celebrating this tree shows how greatness is a matter of quality, not quantity. It does not have the immediacy of some of the grander trees that get Valentines Park 'Notable Collection' status, but what it lacks in stature it makes up for in character. This tree is best seen close up, as from a distance it looks like its most basic description: a small tree. The trunk appears active – riven and twisting, with bits leaning on and around other bits, old sprouting lumps, and younger branches making fortuitous use of spaces created by cuts. The broad base splits low down into a perfect 'v' for sitting in; myth has it that passing a young child through the branches of a field maple gives long life and good health to that child. This 'v' is perfect for that, so take a child along if you can.

The tree was planted in the 17th century, one of a line of trees as hedging, and today's shape gives us the backstory. The trunk is so busy, and the crown a bit lopsided, listing slightly, because the tree was pollarded a lot in its time for its fine-grained wood, which was valued for intricate carving. While the wood grain is delicate, the tree itself is not. Age might have taken away some of its potency. It's a kindly old thing, now on its knees, but for a species that was often used as under-planting, this one has done well without the protection of larger trees around or above it.

Valentines Park's lido, demolished in 1995, was sadly not one of its Grade-II listed features, though there are plenty of things in the public space that that did warrant English Heritage listing. But this is a park of parts. To one side, open sports fields. Next, an almost-wild bit, with natural woody paths. Shell-embellished grottoes. A walled garden. Parts that look and feel typically suburban, with the flat, round, uniform flowerbeds that really only look good as circles of colour in aerial shots. A café building with large, metal-framed windows that, along with the Formica booths, give it the air of a neglected seaside café from the 1950s. Some 10,000 people turned up to the opening ceremony for the park in 1907. In those days, it was a big star.

GETTING THERE

Map ㉛
Location Valentines Park, Perth Road, Gants Hill, IG2.
Access The park is open from 8am till dusk.
Transport Gants Hill tube/ 128, 150, 179 bus.
Directions From the station, enter the park via the Cranbrook Road entrance. Follow the pond straight down, keeping to its left. The maple is on the north-eastern edge of the clump of trees at the end of the pond, facing the old football pitch and golf course.

The Fairlop Oak

Quercus robur

What with scurvy, diptheria, smallpox, lack of sanitation and no *Coronation Street*, living in the 18th century seems to have little to commend it. But boy, did they know how to have a fair. On the first Friday in July, thousands of people from all over the East End would flock to Fairlop for a good session of drunken revelry, thanks to a tradition begun by a local landlord named Daniel Day. That first July Friday was his rent-collection day, and in around 1720 he invited 30 or 40 fellows to meet under the Fairlop oak and eat some celebratory beans and bacon. The girth of the tree at that time was said to be around 30 feet, with a massive canopy of around ten times that. It would have made a phenomenal sight. Day's day grew in size to become a major fair, and by the mid 18th century, more than 100,000 people were coming to carouse there. The tree was old and knackered even by 1767, when Day was buried in a coffin made out of a fallen limb. It was burnt, hollow, broken – and finally blew down, aged around 500 years, in 1820.

   The world marched on. Progress got made. Partying became illegal without a licence, and fairs of any size got a corporate sponsor and a huge entry fee. Some 130 years after the original Fairlop oak hit the ground, in 1951, a new Fairlop oak was planted, partly in remembrance of the old, and partly as a commemoration of the Festival of Britain. But there is no recorded celebratory eating of beans and bacon under this new tree.

   Put aside the romanticism of history: the new Fairlop oak, a common *Quercus robur* like its predecessor, just can't be as good as the original, because of its situation. Where the old sat in Hainault Forest, this sits a couple of miles west, on a large flat traffic roundabout at the end of a long, flat local high street that seems to have missed the last 20 years, but is, at least, not dominated by chains. This is not the place to discover your inner tree-hugger, because you are positively discouraged from approaching the tree by way of grey metal railings, and, oh yes, cars whizzing round. Being planted in 1953 makes the tree not just young in tree years, but young in people years. It's solid looking, healthy... just not particularly exciting; the flatness of the locale seems to pervade the whole atmosphere. Maybe in an attempt to 'create' a landmark through sheer determination, the tree is wrapped in thousands of tiny lights, which by day look like a nasty infestation of strange moth cocoons. The really inspiring thing about this tree is the memory of the old one, so it might be worth timing a visit for the first Friday of July, to see what your mind can conjure up.

GETTING THERE

Map ㉜
Location Fullwell Cross roundabout, High Street, Ilford, Essex IG6 2JP.
Access On a roundabout on a busy public road junction, accessible at all times (but take care crossing).
Transport Fairlop tube/150, 167, 169, 462 bus.
Directions Turn right out of Fairlop station and head along Forest Road. The oak is about 200 yards ahead in the middle of the roundabout.

The Valence Park Holm Oak

Quercus ilex

The benefits of open-air swimming are many, varied and well documented. There are a few lidos left in London, and dedicated swimmers have been known to attempt the lot in one long wet day. A depressing version of that tour, if enjoyment and exercise are anathema to you, is to visit parks where there used to be a lido but it's been filled in. Valence Park is one such venue, and would generally suit a Pessimists' Day Out. The holm oak stands next to a hopeless turgid pond, fenced in by shabby metal railings. The ducks look despondent and unloved. Men sit around fishing, their gloomy shoulders acknowledging this to be a fairly pointless way to pass the day. The council have fixed signs showing a man scarpering with a fish under his arm, with a big red line through it; no scarpering with fish.

Given all that, the tree is great. This is one you have to go *into*, under its cover – the branches dip down almost to the ground, providing a perfect umbrella around the massive trunk. When you pass through this curtain the tree has created, you can hide within a space that has its own microclimate – dry when it's raining, cold when it's warm. The huge trunk splits into five sections right from the ground; heavy dark branches that lean over, out and up.

This is a naturalised tree, as distinct from a native. The latter is one that has always grown in Britain, the naturalised version has been introduced but now is common and established. The evergreen holm is also known as the holly oak, with leaves that resemble those of the holly, only with the sharp edges shaved off. The leaves start off as quite a shiny bright green, then darken with age; underneath they are pale and downy. The tree produces catkins and – it is an oak – acorns. It's often used as a coastal tree because it tolerates salt spray.

Valence Park has the required old house (now a museum) and moat. But the area of Becontree, where Valence Park sits, has a social history that's just as valid. Becontree Estate was built in the 1920s as 'Homes for Heroes', to house soldiers returning home after World War I. It was one of the largest public housing developments in the world, with 27,000 houses and a population of around 100,000. Having an inside toilet was an improvement to people's lives, but the area is not without contention and poverty: the phrase 'corned beef city' – meaning a large council estate – was first coined for this estate, as it was said that this was the only type of food that the inhabitants could afford. The estate was governed by strict rules – a list of preferred plants for front gardens, and privet hedges cut to regulation height, for instance. Social and architectural historians still poke and prod around the place today, while the list of famous people born on the estate includes an unnaturally high proportion of footballers, an ex-Archbishop of Canterbury, and Max Bygraves.

GETTING THERE

Map ㉝

Location Valence Park, Becontree Avenue, Dagenham, RM8.
Access The park gates are open from dawn to dusk.
Transport Chadwell Heath rail/ 5, 62 bus.
Directions Turn right out of the station into Station Road leading to Valence Avenue. At the crossroads with Green Lane, turn left then right into Bonham Road. Turn left into Becontree Avenue from where you enter Valence Park on the right. After 30 yards, take the gate on the right into the pond enclosure. The Holm oak is 20 yards ahead, to the left of the pond.

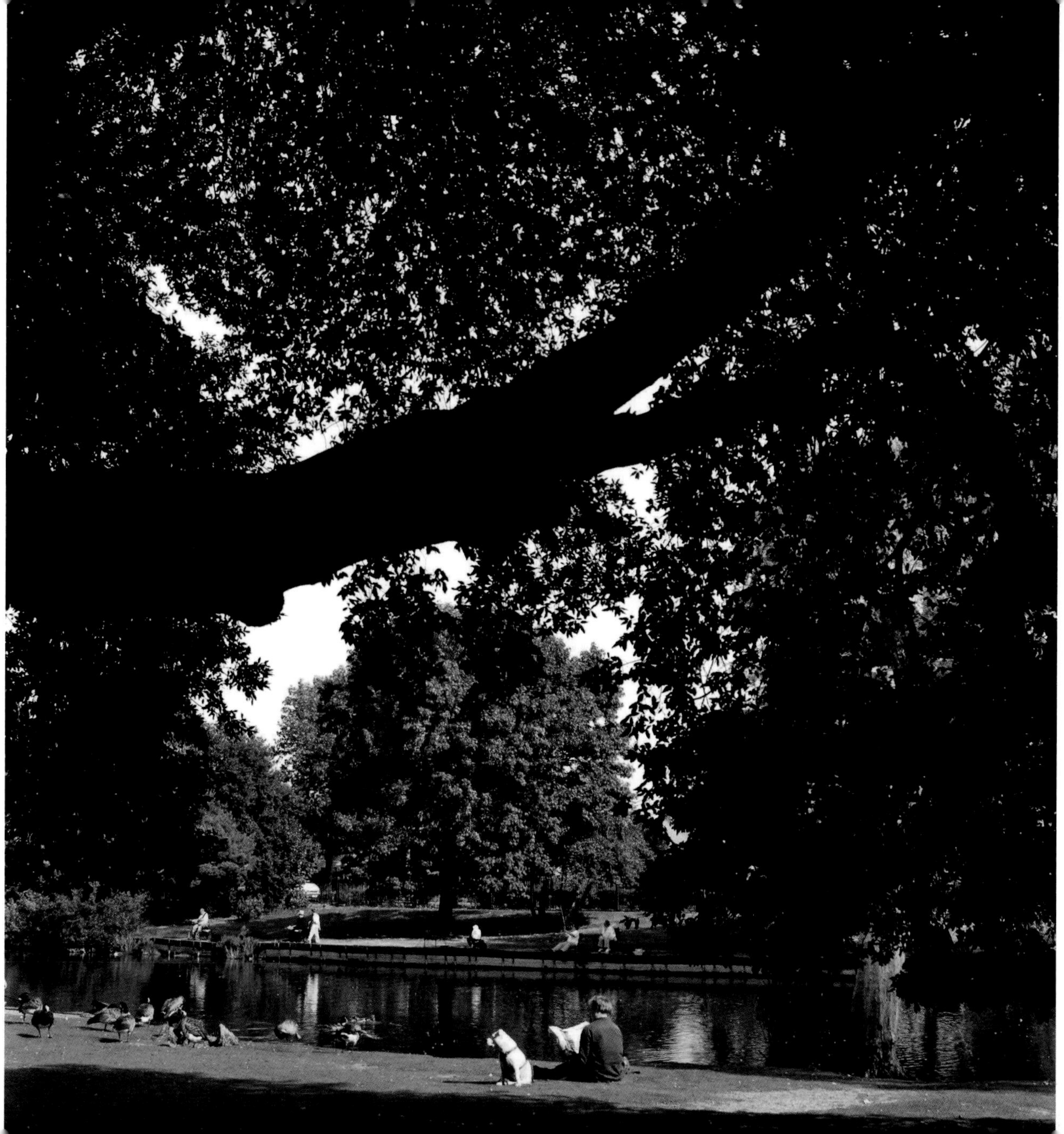

The Valence Park Holm Oak

North

The Amwell Fig

Ficus carica

God, water and property developers: an unlikely alliance, but all are characters in this fig's story. For a start, the tree is actually three trees – a trinity! – three distinct and separate trunks whose branches and foliage have grown together to form one crown. There are figs aplenty in the Bible's New Testament, in parables and as the first items of clothing, so they're often symbolically planted in places of Christian worship. This one is in the small yard at the side of Clerkenwell Parochial Church of England School, one of the oldest purpose-built schools in London, which dates from 1828, fitting well with the estimated age – 200 years – of the fig tree.

As for water... Amwell Street today consists of a row of lovely Georgian houses and an odd mix of bijou shops. It doesn't feel like a destination – more the way to somewhere else. It wasn't always like that. At the northern end of the street, where it joins Pentonville Road, is a bona fide slice of London history: a reservoir (now covered) that formed part of the early attempts to bring water to London residents. From 1609-13, a 40-mile aqueduct was built from the Hertfordshire village of Amwell, giving the street its name and the people a clean water source. From here, it was distributed to a wider community, via hollowed-out elm trunks – an amazing feat. This whole area of Islington was generally known for its walks, spas and tea gardens. An enterprising Mr Sadler discovered a well in the garden of his theatre; as Walter Thornbury writes in 1872, 'The discovery was trumpeted in a pamphlet, detailing the virtues of the water... The Wells soon became famous with hypochondriacs.'

The final part of the trio are property developers. When the site behind this tree was being developed in the early 2000s, the developers carefully incorporated the tree into plans and gave it a long-overdue pruning. It was given a health check, and declared well and vigorous. A popular local feature, it's found on a small triangle of listed school space right beside the pavement, and is making its best effort to colonise the whole area and reach out to passers-by. The tree is resting its weary limbs as it grows away from the back wall behind it; the sloping thick trunks are propped up on four giant green A-shaped supports, like a tree molten. It is lovely, soft, buttery-branched. The trunks are noded and nobbly from pruning cuts, and planted beneath them are spring bulbs – it's the only time of year that anything can flourish underneath, as rain or sun can't penetrate the dense cover once leaves appear. Fig trees become heavy with their own output, with large three-fingered hands of leaves and green-to-brown figs popping out like dusty, round boiled sweets. Fig trees in this country can produce fruit, but in general they only ripen in full sun, which our climate doesn't quite accommodate (yet). Here, the fruit mostly drops, wasted and 'messy' in the way nature is, with no respect for street cleanliness.

GETTING THERE

Map 34

Location Next to the Clerkenwell Parochial Church of England Primary School, Amwell Street, Islington, EC1R 1UN.

Access Just off a public road and accessible at all times.

Transport Angel tube/19, 38, 341 bus.

Directions Turn left out of the station and across Pentonville Road. Take the next right into Myddelton Square. Keeping to the left of the square, head straight down River Street, then turn left on to Amwell Street. The fig tree is on the other side of the road, just before Margery Street.

The Totteridge Yew

Taxus baccata

'In this churchyard is a yew tree of a very remarkable size, its girth, at three feet from the ground, being 26 feet'. So said Dr S Lysons in 1796 – over 200 years ago. Finding it hard to imagine Totteridge 200 years ago? Then chew on this: the very tree Dr S was writing about was already 1,800 years old by then. Now, aged around 2,000 years, it's the oldest tree in London. The vicar even has a signed certificate from Professor David Bellamy of the Conservation Foundation to say so. And that (the age, not the signature) is boggling, by anyone's standards.

This tree is a special sight. It's a sprightly ancient: age might have battered it, but expert management has ensured that it still has vigorous new growth. It's not tall, which goes some way to explaining its age, as it's less likely to be blown over in a storm. But it makes up for its shortness with that very chunky girth, still at around 26 feet. It has a short, hollowed inner trunk, surrounded by wide, low limbs that protect the inner platform. The shaggy unevenness of the branches hides what goes on within, and when you creep in to look, you see how incredibly textured the aged wood is – sometimes resembling dark contorted limbs as painted by Egon Schiele, sometimes like a sun-dried piece of rock when the tide has gone out, leaving the marks of limpets and whelks. The outer branches continue to provide the yew with the lush permanent growth of an evergreen, with its tough needle-leaf. It sits right by the front gate of the village church of St Andrew's, and has one large square tomb underneath and several smaller ones now subsumed by the ground.

This yew has a part to play in village history. It used to be the venue for the village's hundred courts (a hundred was an ancient territorial division, so this was an early version of a local magistrates court, probably dealing with unruly youth even then). It even had a baby abandoned in its shelter in 1722, named Henry Totteridge.

While each old beauty has its own story, yew trees are also fantastic repositories of this country's history. The placing of this one is significant in that respect. For ancient Celts, they were used in ritual as symbols of immortality – yews are pretty difficult to kill, as this one amply demonstrates. Many are found in churchyards, but often pre-date the church building, as in this case. This one is being helped along into its next century: 30-odd years ago, experts from Kew Gardens came and loosened the soil around the roots, judiciously cut it, and poured hardening material into the heart of the tree to prevent it drying out too much.

The 'ridge' of Totteridge is high and dry, with panoramic views. Wealthy merchants took advantage of this preferred land in the 15th and 16th centuries, and the huge, gated driveways suggest that nothing has changed in that respect. It's the kind of place where the one real surprise is a bus stop. Public transport? Only for staff, surely.

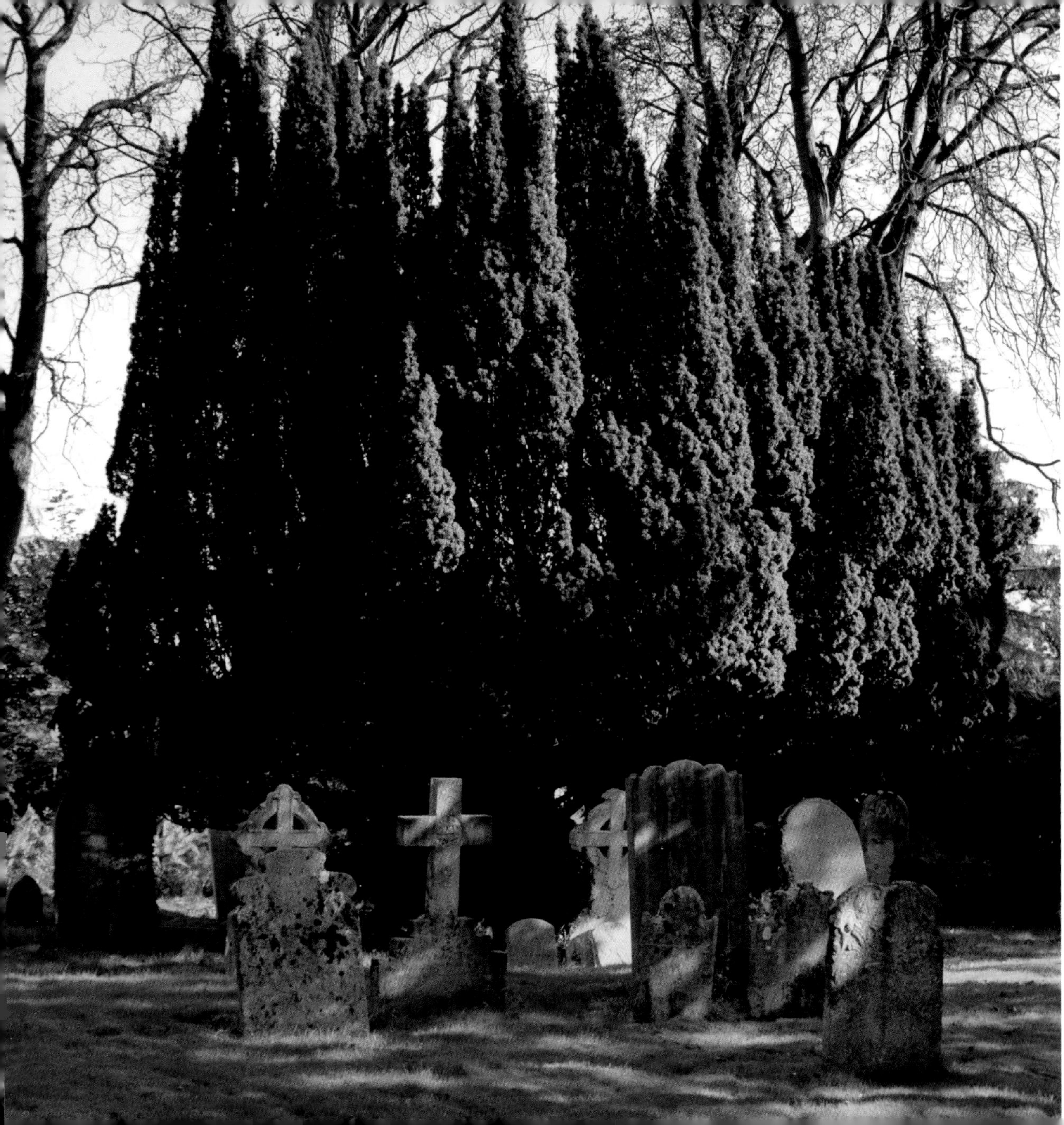

The Totteridge Yew

Species watch Yew

An ancient and sacred tree with a remarkably lengthy lifespan.

The oldest yew in Britain – in Fortingall, Scotland – is somewhere between 3,000 and 5,000 years old. Because of the way yews grow, with new trunks forming around the heartwood as it splits and rots in our damp climate, precise dating is impossible. There are no rings to count. But even at the most conservative estimate, this is the oldest tree in Europe, and cuttings are being taken to give it a horizon beyond the churchyard in which it lives.

Trees such as the Fortingall Yew, and the yews in this book, are critically important because of their historical and social significance, and exciting by the simple fact of their age. There are dedicated groups giving care and attention to the most ancient of them (look for the Ancient Yew Group). Yews had enormous sacred significance for Celts, representing the delicate journey to the underworld on death, and Druids, for whom it is the tree of eternity. It makes sense that a long-living evergreen tree should symbolise nature's power to regenerate.

More than 80 per cent of the yews in Britain can be found in churchyards, giving the church an important custodial role for this living history. They survive well in churchyards because ancient woodland, where it still exists, doesn't offer the same level of physical and climatic protection. However, many of the yews pre-date their churchyard homes – a common theory is that Christians built on pagan ceremonial sites, thus inheriting the trees therein. That sounds like good business practice; if you're going to introduce a new religion, offering a few tokens of similarity would help ease people from one to the other. For early Christians, the yew was associated with the resurrection, and yew branches were used on Palm Sunday in the days before exotic palms were an option here.

It seems oddly appropriate that a tree so associated with the ceremonial rites around life and death is actually poisonous in most of its parts. Indeed, the planting of yew trees in burial grounds, and as hedges, may have been to deter farmers from grazing livestock there. The bright red aril (the fleshy bit around the seed) is not poisonous, but instead has laxative qualities (so avoid standing underneath the birds who snack on it). The wood of the tree, being slow-growing, is tightly grained and hard. It was perfect for English longbows, and European yew forests were decimated because of the trees felled to arm our medieval armies. Now, the yew is associated with a different type of fight: the bark of the tree contains a chemical called taxol, which is an anti-cancer drug. This has contributed to further yew decimation, giving us extra reason to protect our heritage trees in the UK.

All the facts and stories about yews draw a dramatic picture of a tree at the heart of life and death, right to the present day. Even in their everyday clothes, as hedging and topiary, they have the propensity to be glorious. Yews also inspire people partly because of how they look; if they were straight up-and-down, would we find them so compelling? Instead, the form these ancient individual specimens take – full of cracks and hollows new and old, and twists and turns – can be inspirational, and great for hide-and-seek or storytelling in whatever century you find them.

The Hendon Japanese Maple

Acer palmatum

There is something refined about Japanese maples, which makes one raise one's descriptive game. They are very distinctive trees, often planted for the autumn colour of their foliage, which is, indeed, splendid. The filigree leaves provide a blazing ball of colour, from the darkest purple to fizzing cherryade red or an almost fluorescent yellow. But it's also worth visiting in spring for the lift it can give you. The piercing, almost lime green of the new leaves as they begin to appear against the bright fuchsia pink of the leaf stems makes the tree look like a work of hazy pixellation, with an acid shimmer so fashionable it could be a piece of contemporary design. On one of those days when the temperatures start to rise, when you can actually feel a tiny bit of warmth from the sun, the tree presents a refreshing hit of colour, with the kind of intensity you can practically taste. It's a hopeful treat.

There are thousands of different cultivars of *Acer palmatum*; they've become a byword for elegance, a sophisticated example of grace in nature. They're used as 'accent' trees (trees planted on the borders to complete the picture), and to provide gentle shade. They're a good fit with the aesthetics of simplicity and ideal beauty of Japanese gardening. There's no such thing as instant Zen, but an *Acer palmatum* helps. They have a sense of subtlety, and though the leaf shape and colour varies considerably, they're always delicate and deeply fingered – often as wispy as tiny pieces of dangling decorative lace. The leaves of this cultivar, the heptalobum, are seven-lobed (hence the hepta) and not laser-cut with such finesse as other cultivars, but good nonetheless. Japanese acers are popular for the strange and beautiful art of bonsai, because they respond well to that kind of full-on pruning and root manipulation. But this one goes to the other size extreme: you see acers everywhere as ornamentals, or at eye-level with shrubby proportions, but this is a really impressive tree, one of the biggest of this species in London.

If the Hendon maple were reproduced in miniature, it would look like a tied bunch of flowers, with a ribbon bringing the stems together into a clutched bunch. The base is buttressed and multi-trunked; at around three feet high, the trunks converge to form a bowl in their centre – literally, as it can fill with rainwater. The many limbs coming off that bowl open out again and rise up, growing to produce a beautiful dome crown. It sits in a welcoming position at the top of Hendon Park, which started life as part of a medieval estate, Steps Fields, and came into public ownership in 1903 to be laid out as a formal Edwardian park. That neatly dates the tree, as part of the original planting, to be just over 100 years old. It now sits alone but very distinctively, with branches overhanging the high tennis court fences.

GETTING THERE

Map 36

Location Hendon Park, Queen's Road, Hendon, NW4 4UP.

Access The park gates are never locked, so it's accessible at all times.

Transport Hendon Central tube/ 13, 143, 186, 362, 643, 797 bus.

Directions Turn left out of the station into Queen's Road, which runs back over the railway line. The entrance to the park is on the right. Go past the park café and the first two tennis courts; the maple stands to the right of the path.

The Wembley Elm 🍃

Ulmus laevis

Wembley Stadium's newest incarnation features the arch across north London's skyline, designed by Norman Foster, architect of other London icons such as the Gherkin and the Millennium Bridge. It couldn't fail to become an instant landmark. With that size and scope, you'd imagine it would render anything nearby, like this mere tree, insignificant. And on one hand it does; coming in to Wembley, even flying over it, the arch soars into constant view. Ironically, though, it seems that as you get really close, the stadium gets more hidden. From the nearest tube (Wembley Central) to the tree, the buildings are too high and close to allow sight of the stadium, even though it's only a hefty stone's throw away. Then, turn a corner away from the cheap fried-chicken and pound shops, and the sky opens up. Over the roofs of houses, the arch almost ethereally echoes the curve of the lowest branches of the Wembley Elm. The tree can block your view, or frame it; but seeing the stadium obliquely is almost more revealing than seeing it full frontal. Whatever your take on football, this is an impressive site, the clean white structure resembling a bleached skeleton, and distinct even in the greyest sky.

In a paved area outside a pub, the tree marks the start of something different: respectful suburbia clustering round the monolith of the stadium in the distance. The tree is in good condition: the fissures of the bark nicely mirror the delicate filigree of the many tiny branches coming off the main ones. The tree is noted on the plaque only as 'sp' – elms are renowned for being one of the most difficult genus to narrow down. Since the plaque went up, however, an expert has delineated it as *Ulmus laevis* – a European white elm, or fluttering elm. They thrive in damp conditions, and their trunks are notably buttressed at the base. As this one is dry and not buttressed, it perfectly demonstrates how complicated identification can be. Elms were a popular European ornamental through the 18th and 19th centuries, being really good shade trees and well adapted for their use as street trees because of their spread and the curving nature of the upper branches. This particular tree has been in place for as long as people have been watching the beautiful game in Wembley – so over 100 years. As a small tree, it may have shaded visitors to Watkin's Folly, London's answer to the Eiffel Tower. MP Sir Edward Watkins saw the Parisian tower, and wanted something similar, only taller (natch) for London. Eiffel himself was invited to design it, but declined. It opened in 1894, not even half-built: a cheap, four-legged version, a quarter of the height of the original. Money had run out, and as it was built on marshy foundations, the whole structure was unstable, which wasn't exactly a draw for visitors. It was demolished in 1907.

The tree and arch now both serve a good purpose: they make you lift your head from the pavement and look up. It feels good. And that is clever design.

GETTING THERE

Map ㉗

Location Outside the Greyhound pub, Harrow Road, Wembley, HA9 6LL.
Access On a public road and accessible at all times.
Transport Wembley Stadium rail/ 18, 83 bus.
Directions Leave the station by the main exit and turn left into Wembley Hill Road. Follow the road around a left-hand bend into Harrow Road. The elm is just after this bend, in front of the Greyhound pub.

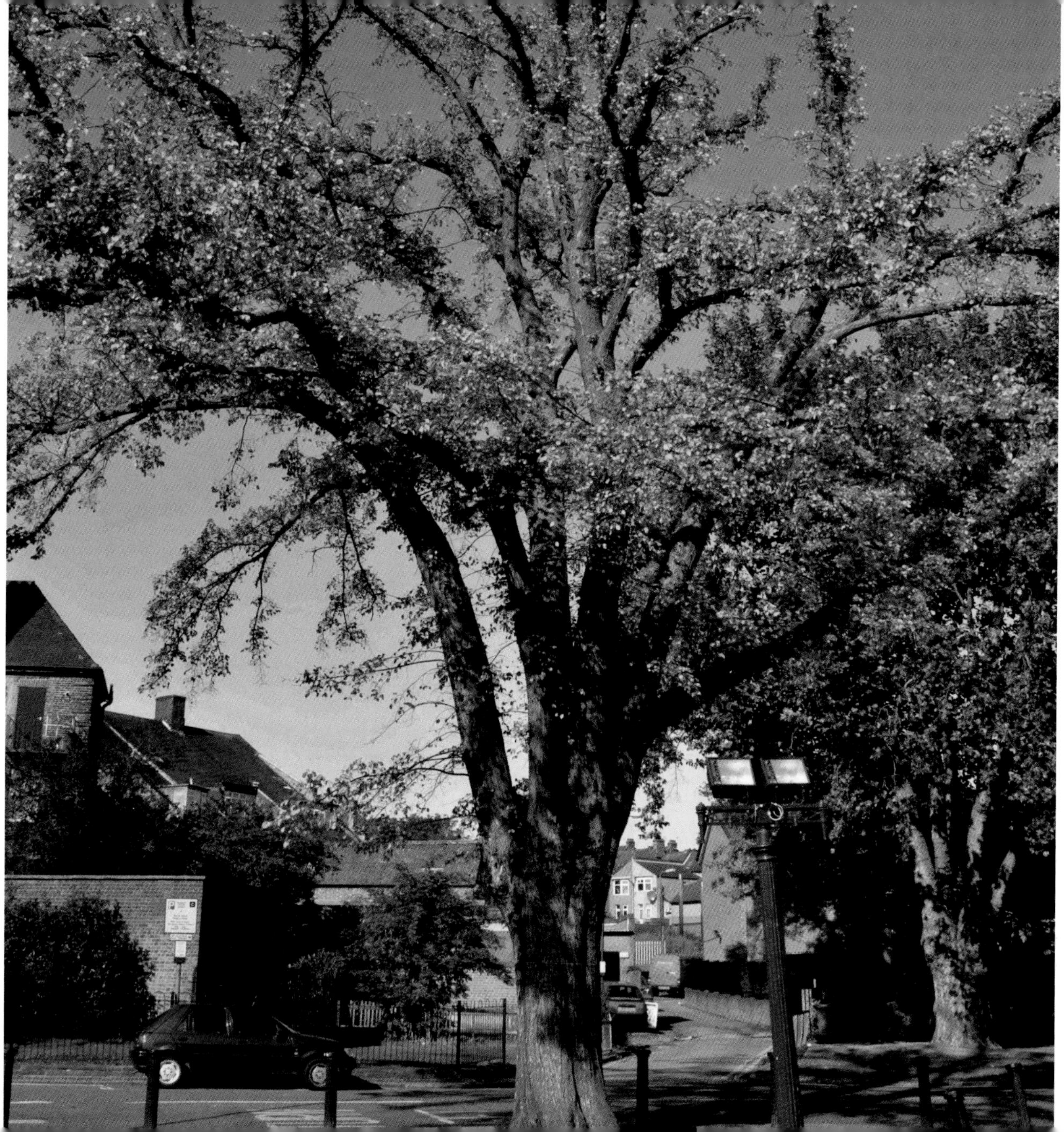

The Wembley Elm

The Forty Hall Cedar of Lebanon

Cedrus libani

Cedars of Lebanon really do know how to make an impression. Their stately stature and shape mean that they make a fantastic specimen tree that can truly dominate the right landscape. This one is stunning in size and scope. If you're of a competitive bent, you might like to know it's a 'Champion cedar' with 'Champion girth', though it probably only garners a silver medal in terms of age – the oldest specimen in Britain has resided at Childrey in Oxfordshire since 1646. This one was planted around the turn of the 18th century, when it would have been a grand statement of fashion and class; as one of the first in London, nay in the country, it's hard to think what tree would be equally awe-inspiring today.

With a huge girth, and massive branches, this is a tree with unavoidable presence. The enormous bole looks solid and weighty, forcefully powering up from the earth, with branches that are themselves as thick as trees coming off close to the base. Where new leaf growth is coming through, a delicate flash of bright acid green tingles at the ends of branches. The cedar has, however, been considerably pruned, with some enormous branches cut off top and bottom. Old photos no longer match the new shape. Now it has a consolidated flat top, a much smaller platform of upper greenery, is more upright and with less symmetry in the spread than before these major amputations. The cuts, their stumps on view, along with an old hollow at the back of the trunk, remind us that this specimen has vulnerabilities; that although it is essentially much more permanent than we individuals are, it remains temporary, surviving thanks to the ministering of good practice and its bulky resistance to natural forces. It remains majesterial, the time for abdication still many years off.

The tree, as well as looking so fabulous, is also perfectly placed right in front of Forty Hall – a Grade-I listed Jacobean Hall built in 1629 as a private residence, now open to the public. The grounds are Grade-II listed, with original walled gardens and a walk of lime trees that was replanted after the storm of 1987. More native planting, and ancient methods of woodland management (basically a lot more coppicing) have been reintroduced, which improve trees' lifespans and the amount of wildlife they attract. Somehow, this all contributes to the feel of the place: there is a sense of serenity to the park. It's beautifully laid out, calm in atmosphere and there's a café... what more could you want? A glass of own-label Pinot, perhaps? Forty Hall Park has a farm with 15 acres of vines from which they aim to make Forty Hall organic wine. This will be the first commercial vineyard in London since medieval times. But it'll take some time for the first bottles to appear; so for now, the capital will have to remain known for consuming, not producing.

GETTING THERE

Map 38

Location Grounds of Forty Hall, Forty Hill, Enfield, EN2 9HA.
Access The grounds are open dawn to dusk daily. The house is open 11am to 4pm Wed to Sun.
Transport Enfield Town or Turkey Street rail/191 bus.
Directions It's a 20-minute walk from Turkey Street station. Exit into Winnington Road veering to the left. Turn right over the railway footbridge. Follow the footpath over the A10, and then along the brook until you reach Forty Hill Road. Turn left and then right into the grounds of Forty Hall House. The cedar is to the left, as you face the house, with the lake behind.

Sowing the seeds of survival

The future for London's trees.

London is lucky. Our trees are protected by a number of bodies from national government downwards (or upwards, depending on where you're standing), and cared for by people who understand that the seven million trees in Greater London are hugely important. The renowned greenness of this city is part of its unique beauty, which in turn contributes to its economic strength via tourism.

The most immediate and pressing problem for London – and its trees – is, without doubt, climate change. As temperatures rise and water becomes a traded commodity, we have to protect what we have, and plan for the future. It's essential that everyone, from the private garden owners responsible for 20 per cent of London's land cover, to the managers of our largest parks, maintains older trees for their efficacy in carbon exchange, and plants new trees to help deal with the extremes of temperature in the future. Of course, trees can't save us from ourselves; one, two, even 20 or 30 trees down each street won't offset the need to stop depending on fossil fuels. But they can help, in real ways, with the problems this dependence has created – for instance, through filtering pollution, shading buildings and people and thus creating cooler streets, helping with water run-off and noise pollution. More than ever, trees are integral to modern, open-space planning, and integral to the well-being of city dwellers.

Trees also have the spectre of pests and diseases. Is it possible to foresee what nasty attackers are headed this way? No, is the simple answer; there is no prediction, only careful management. If the London plane, for instance, fell prey to something on the scale of Dutch Elm Disease, the city would be irrevocably altered; devastated beyond imagination. Trees are affected by fungal, bacterial or viral diseases, and there are several on the hot-list for concern. A new pathogen, a variant of sudden oak death that has caused major problems in the US, has been identified in Cornwall; bleeding canker of the horse chestnut is not new, but is on the increase. The names might have a Dickensian quality, but the problems the diseases pose are certainly not fictional. Similarly with pests; the oak processionary moth was first spotted in Britain along the A40 near Sheen in 2006; the caterpillars can defoliate a tree, which obviously then affects its ability to photosynthesise. For the past few years, horse chestnuts, especially in southern England, have been ravaged by the leaf miner moth; by July, the leaves have turned brown and shrivelled, as if autumn had come early.

Biodiversity is key to the success of our future treescape. The people living here are not mono-cultural, so actually being diverse is integral to London. But it's more than a social reflection. Biodiversity makes financial sense for tree management – if different trees need different things at different times, resources can be spread out. If one disease hits, not everything will suffer. Biodiversity supports more wildlife, and better conserves existing wildlife. In uncertain climate times, planting a diverse range of trees means there's a better chance that some will do well. And if we acknowledge that trees instinctively make people happy (which we surely do), looking at a group of different trees, of all colours, sizes and shapes is a stimulating, inspiring sight. One tree type dominating the landscape is not healthy, or natural. And healthy nature makes the city a better place to be, on every level.

The Forty Hall Cedar of Lebanon

British native trees

This list doesn't include trees such as the London plane or the horse chestnut. These have become commonplace and may be considered typically British because they've been in the country for centuries, but they are naturalised, rather than native. Native trees are usually defined as those that have inhabited Britain since the end of the last Ice Age; naturalised trees have been introduced (deliberately or accidentally) and gone on to successfully establish themselves, reproducing naturally in the wild and spreading.

The Latin species name often relates to some of the tree's natural features.

Field maple
Acer campestre
Our only native maple (*below and above*). Sycamores are of the same family but not native, and often scorned as weeds.

Alder
Alnus glutinosa
Small, usually found in damp places; been in Britain for around 9,000 years. New leaves are sticky and glutinous.

Strawberry tree
Arbutus unedo
Native to south-west Ireland. The fruit might look like small strawberries, but they definitely don't taste like them.

Silver birch
Betula pendula
Very common and revered for its elegant white bark. Short-lived.

Downy or white birch
Betula pubescens
The Latin name means, rather sweetly, 'finely hairy'. Similar to silver birch, but without black diamond patterns on the trunk.

Box
Buxus sempervirens
This tree only just made it as a native. Often seen as a shrub, topiarised or as hedging. Slow-growing and very smelly.

Hazel
Corylus avellana
A very common woodland tree, but really shrub-like. Early tribes in Britain would have survived on the nuts.

Hornbeam
Carpinus betulus
Part of the birch family; cultivars are often planted in parks and streets.

Common hawthorn
Crataegus monogyna
The *very* common hawthorn, also known as 'May' due to the white blossom that usually appears in that month.

Midland hawthorn
Crataegus laevigata
Looks like a pinky-red flowering version of the hawthorn. A common street tree.

Beech
Fagus sylvatica
The Latin name means 'of the woods'. It's noted for its elegance, and its beautiful golden-brown autumnal leaves.

Ash
Fraxinus excelsior
Its black buds help in its identification. The fourth commonest tree species in Britain.

Holly
Ilex aquifolium
Evergreen, with iconic bright red berries and spiny foliage. A very common species.

Common juniper
Juniperus communis
Breathe in: the female plant berries are used to flavour gin.

Crab apple
Malus sylvestris
'Crab' means producing a sour fruit, not a sweet one. Thorny too.

Scots pine
Pinus sylvestris
The only pine native to Britain – the only true native pine forest being in the Scottish Highlands.

Aspen
Populus tremula
A poplar. The leaves famously 'quiver' as their long, slender leaf stalks flutter in the breeze.

Black poplar
Populus nigra
Featured in Constable paintings, but now rare. It has a dark trunk with lots of swollen burrs. Known as the Manchester poplar in the same way the London plane is identified with the capital.

Wild cherry
Prunus avium
Ornamental, white flowers in spring, followed by sour red fruit.

Bird cherry
Prunus padus
A small tree, found mainly in the south as a specimen, but also grows wild in the north of England, Scotland and Ireland.

English oak
Quercus robur
One of the most significant native trees in British history, and the predominant timber tree since prehistoric times. *Pictured above and below left and right.*

Sessile oak
Quercus petraea
Called 'sessile' because the acorns are without stalks. Taller than the English oak, where the acorns do have stalks.

British native trees (continued)

▶ **Crack willow**
Salix fragilis
Easily broken, as both the common and
Latin names indicate – a twig will snap
off with a crack.

Goat willow
Salix caprea
The famous 'pussy willow', the most
common willow. Native everywhere
in Britain, except the Outer Hebrides.

Bay willow
Salix pentandra
The bay willow has five stamens, as
the Latin name suggests. A streamside
grower, from North Wales upwards.
Its leaves resemble bay leaves.

White willow
Salix alba
Part of the classic country river view;
famously used to make cricket bats.

Rowan
Sorbus aucuparia
The highest-growing deciduous tree;
its pinnate leaves look like ash, hence
the common name of mountain ash.

Whitebeam
Sorbus aria
A southern English species, with
leaves that are white underneath;
mostly a street tree.

True service tree
Sorbus domestica
Meaning 'used around the house',
but for what is not clear. A species
of rowan.

Wild service tree
Sorbus torminalis
'Torminalis' means good for colic, but
in the past, the fruits were preferred
when made into alcoholic drinks.

Common yew
Taxus baccata
Outlives many others; often found in
churchyards. It has toxic seeds and
foliage. *Pictured below.*

Small leaf lime
Tilia cordata
Small, heart-shaped leaves and bright,
starry flowers. It buzzes with insects
when in full bloom.

Broad leaf lime
Tilia platyphyllos
Shorter than the common lime, and
not as widespread. It's known as the
Linden tree in Germany.

Wych elm
Ulmus glabra
Wych meaning pliant, or switchy,
this is the only elm that can set seed,
meaning produce seed after flowering.

South

The Battersea Park Hybrid Strawberry Tree

Arbutus x andrachnoides

If you're a collector of tree-related accolades, this one is for you: this tree has the stoutest girth of any hybrid strawberry tree in the British Isles. Admittedly, that's not a huge group from which to emerge victorious; this Greek native is described as an 'infrequent' species, which makes it neither rare nor common. But if its bulging girth isn't enough to send you racing to see it, we offer some more reasons.

The most striking thing about the tree is the bark. It's a paprika-red brown, peeling in long, brandy-snap curls. That colour, combined with the bulging base, the twisting trunk and the hunched-over branches make this a great witchy tree under which to tell scary stories. Autumn is thus a perfect time to visit; and even though the tree's leaf, girth and bark remain the same all year, its surroundings are really splendid at that time. Battersea Park was created as an arboretum, a showcase of trees collected from around the world by Victorian plant hunters, and our tree may have been one of the originals; it certainly dates from the late 1850s. The park, last renovated in 2004, has 170 species of tree in its 200 acres, which give a display of stunning autumnal leaf colour and fantastic emergent structural shapes. Which makes this south London park a worthy spot in which to celebrate the seasonal glory of all London tree species – even specimens not officially 'great'.

Battersea Park was originally laid out as a place where people could get lost, and, in the hunt for the hybrid strawberry tree, does not disappoint. Large areas of the park offer stylised avenues and flat, open vistas, but this tree nestles on a narrow path around a collection of ponds in the southern section of the park. It's on the edge of the Ladies Pond (though there's no signage of that name) – so-called, perhaps, because it's a smaller adjunct to the main lake. In the same way they would have done 150 years ago, the lanes twist and turn, up and over bridges and humps. And then, on a dark, dense bend, banked up inside some black railings, squats our tree, Buddha-broad at its base, the trunk reaching up to the light and some branches twisting across over the path and our heads. It is evergreen, but the leaf cover looks a little sparse; it has lost some of its vigour, which may be climate-related or, perhaps, as an over-mature tree, it just deserves a break. It bears tiny, unprepossessing panicles of white flowers in autumn, but they are hard to spot on anything other than the very lowest branches, and certainly not worth bringing a stepladder for. This is a naturally occurring hybrid of the strawberry tree, *Arbutus unedo*, and the Greek strawberry tree, *A. andrachne*. If you had the image of a tree dripping with succulent berries, the *unedo* is a clue to the tree's fruit – the derivation means 'I eat one', as in, 'I won't make that mistake twice'.

GETTING THERE

Map ㊴

Location North-west side of the lake, Battersea Park, Battersea, SW11. The nearest entrance is on Queenstown Road.

Access The park gates are open from 8am to dusk.

Transport Battersea Park rail/ 44, 49, 137, 319, 344, 345 bus.

Directions From the station, turn right, then right again into Queenstown Road; walk towards the roundabout and enter the park from the opposite side. Once in the park, turn left and follow the path closest to the lake on the right, until you see a sculpture of three figures on the left. Turn right; the tree is on your right at the second bend. Look for the red-orange bark and convoluted trunk.

LONDON TREE FORUM WWW.FORESTRY.GOV.UK

HYBRID STRAWBERRY TREE
THE BIGGEST IN BRITAIN (1997),
ONE OF THE
GREAT TREES OF LONDON

ARBUTUS X ANDRACHOIDES

THIS PLAQUE IS SUPPORTED BY ESSO UK PLC
FOR TREES OF TIME AND PLACE

The Tate Plane

Platanus x hispanica

Don't take a bottle of wine to drink by this tree, because you'll get arrested. The Tate Gardens might sound fancy, but the space is designated an 'alcohol control zone' for reasons that are obvious if you're familiar with the area. Don't take too many expectations from the word 'gardens' either. Think more 'busy road junction' and you'll be less disappointed. A short walk from Brixton tube, the tree is at the meeting point of Acre Lane, Coldharbour Lane, Effra Road and Brixton Road: it's a good job planes are resistant to pollution. On a more progressive note, the immediate area features Windrush Square, commemorating the first West Indian immigrants to arrive in this country on the boat of that name.

The Tate plane has become something of a landmark, an additional signpost outside two iconic buildings – the Ritzy cinema and Brixton library. The tree, library and the 'gardens' are named after industrialist Henry Tate, who lived in nearby Streatham in the late 1800s. Famously associated with art galleries, we should thank him on a more prosaic level for giving us the sugar cube. It's beyond the remit of this book to wonder 'where would we be without the sugar cube', but the answer is probably not Brixton.

The nutshell history of this tiny corner of south-west London takes us from the earliest days of grass-grazing, when it was sheep pasture. The library was built in 1893, Brixton Theatre a year later; the theatre's foundation stone was laid by famous actor Henry Irving, and now rests at the edge of the garden area. The cinema arrived in 1910, then one of nine in the area and known as the Electric Pavilion; the Tate Library garden would then have been fancy. Through a posh wrought-iron gate into the enclosed landscaping, a bust of Henry Tate sat proudly on a twirled, wedding cake-style pillar, in one of the raised flower beds circled by tiny hoops of fencing. The plane was probably planted in the 1920s, and survived when the theatre didn't, destroyed by bombs in 1940.

Now at least 80 years old, the tree sits in the ubiquitous urban canvas: a little bit of uninspiring flat lawn, much slabbing and ramps, rounded red-brick walls designed to be uncomfortably low to sit on unless you're a toddler. Not a bench in sight, because that might encourage loitering, with or without intent. But bland modern planning has actually served our tree pretty well, and shows how important it is locally. Even the bust of Tate himself has been demoted to give the tree pole position – his plinth looks rather lonely and outdated stuck off to the side. The tree, as is appropriate for something with centre-stage status, is clearly a very healthy specimen. It has a balanced crown with plenty of room to spread fully, and a robust trunk. It's lit with lightbulbs twined through the branches in winter months, giving a nice twinkly counterpoint to that complex, usually blocked road system.

152 Time Out The Great Trees of London

GETTING THERE

Map ⓵

Location Outside Tate Library, Brixton Oval, Coldharbour Lane, Lambeth, SW2 1JQ.

Access On public land and accessible at all times.

Transport Brixton tube/rail/ 2, 3, 35, 45, 59, 133, 159 bus.

Directions Turn left from the station on to Brixton Road. The tree is straight ahead, 150 yards away.

The Brockwell Oak

Quercus robur

'A society grows great when old men plant trees whose shade they know they shall never sit in.' A Greek proverb that's worth transplanting to south-west London, when considering the lifespan of the Brockwell Oak.

Accounts differ: some say it is 500 years old, others that it's closer to 700. Either way, this tree existed long before the building of Brockwell Hall, on whose grand sweep of a lawn it has sat for some 200 years. Up until the mid 1500s, part of what is now Brockwell Park was the grounds of a monastic order; this tree thus being one of a boundary line of trees probably planted and definitely tended by medieval monks. The proverb raises a reflection: in planting this tree, was theirs a great society? And by extension, in caring for it and celebrating its survival and heritage, is ours also great? The tree remains a constant, but the changes that have passed around it really stretch the imagination: from being on the edge of a large tract of rural woodland, to shading the monks as they went about their business, and finally being a celebrated focus in a popular urban park – and everything that came between those great leaps in time. All of that is readable in one trunk if you stop and look long enough.

This English oak is a fabulous beast. A huge girth of over 20 feet helps to identify it as ancient, and that kind of proportion gives it venerable status. Its size dwarfs a mere mortal – the fissures are large enough to put a fist in. The detail of its knobbles and bumps are like a troll's face, positively alive with features – the twisted nose, the lumpy craggy chin, the boils and warts bulging. At chest-height the trunk appears to slump down on itself, become ridged, like a rucked-up cardigan on an old person. Trees, like people, do shrink with age. This tree has a massive spread of branches, remaining vigorous and reaching upward. It's still supporting wildlife in the way it did in medieval times; then it would have been pigs, now it's more prosaic – insects, birds and squirrels.

The tree is in the south-east corner of the park, on a grass slope running downhill from the front of Brockwell Hall. The house was built in 1811, as the country seat of a London gentleman, quite an incongruous image given that the surrounding housing, traffic and trains make it feel very far from the countryside. When to go and see it? Try a sunny day between May and September, and take your swimming stuff: Brockwell Park is home to an unheated lido, one of few remaining in the capital. The joys of outdoor swimming are well documented, as are the health benefits of cold water – but that's a topic for another book.

GETTING THERE

Map ⑪

Location South-east side of Brockwell Park, Herne Hill, SE24.
Access The park gates are open from 7.30am to dusk.
Transport Herne Hill rail/ 3, 37, 68, 196, 322, 468 bus.
Directions Take the station's left exit, then turn right into the park, crossing Dulwich Road. Take the middle path towards Brockwell Hall. Go round to the front of the hall, past the path going downhill, and the oak stands alone, 20 yards ahead and to the left.

Species watch Oak

A species that's played a starring role in England's heritage.

From tiny acorns mighty oaks do grow: these trees have inspired authors from Thomas Carlyle to Rudyard Kipling and Shakespeare – Macbeth's Birnam Wood was full of oaks, and both the original Globe Theatre and its replacement are oak buildings. The oak is the tree both of kings (Charles II took refuge in one) and vagabonds (Robin Hood reputedly lived in an oak in Sherwood Forest, with room for a few merry men, one can suppose). The Bowthorpe Oak in Lincoln is estimated to be Britain's oldest oak at over 1,000 years; the nature of oaks means that they often hollow with age, and this one is large enough to host a party within its trunk.

There is something quintessentially English about the oak; because it's our main forest tree, it has been instrumental in the shaping of our industry, landscape and pub names. Oak is a strong, durable wood, easy to work with and capable of producing very long timbers – and we've made the most of it. Our timber-framed homes and ships used oak, and 18th-century landowners were persuaded that planting oaks was part of their patriotic duty to keep the Navy furnished with building materials. The Houses of Parliament has lovely old oak panelling contributing to its sense of importance, and Portcullis House, the newest parliamentary building, is oak-panelled, as befits our expensive MPs.

There are around 500 species of oak – some deciduous, some evergreen, not all with that typical blunt wavy leaf shape. The two natives are the English (common, or pedunculate) and the sessile. The English, *Quercus robur*, meaning robust and strong, thrives in the heavier soils of the south of England, while the sessile, *Quercus petraea*, roams the north more freely. They can be distinguished by the way their acorns hang: pedunculate acorns are on a long stalk and the leaves are practically stalkless; it's the other way round on the sessile oak. That's a fine distinction, and the trees hybridise freely in forests, so it's not always a possible one to call.

Oaks remain incredibly important: they host more species of wildlife than any other tree – from bats, birds and insects to mosses, lichen and fungi. The young leaves and acorns contain tannic acid, though, which is poisonous to horses, and addictive: the equine equivalent of a smoking habit.

Gospel Oak doesn't just refer to the place in north London; other villages also had their 'gospel oak', where the gospel was preached in the shade of a large tree. The oak is associated with plenty of other tribes, from Greeks and Celts to Druids. There's a fantastic collection of folkloric tales around the tree; when Christ was going to be crucified, legend has it that all the trees got together and decided to split, rendering themselves unusable for a cross. Only the holly oak remained unsplit – the traitor! Oaks are seen as portals to other worlds, and carrying an acorn can prevent you from getting old. 'Fairy folk live in oak,' it's said, and they like to come into your house through the knotholes in oak floorboards.

The Lewisham Dutch Elm

Ulmus x hollandica 'Klemmer'

This tree brings up an interesting situation. Two other elms have made Great Tree status, which, considering how Dutch Elm Disease absolutely decimated elms here and across Europe, the US and Canada, is pretty good going – although it could be that their relative rarity in our landscape helped them become 'Great'. The Marylebone Elm (*see p34*) is a Huntingdon elm; the Wembley Elm (*see p138*) was initially noted as *Ulmus* 'Sp' but later identified as *Ulmus laevis*. And therein lies the problem with elms, the species absolutely designed for obsessives. There are lists, lists and lists: there are hybrids, cultivars and hybrid-cultivars, synonyms, species and varieties – enough to make you wish you had a tree degree, or at least a big dictionary before you begin. Then there are the cultivars of unconfirmed derivation, of which this elm is one; a perfect lesson in obfuscation.

It's definitely recorded as *Ulmus x hollandica* 'Klemmer'. It's also known as *Ulmus* 'Klemmer', or the Flanders elm. Which means that it's a Dutch elm that's probably a natural hybrid between a Wych elm (*Ulmus glabra*) and a Field elm (*Ulmus minor*). It's only 'probably' because elms hybridise very easily, which makes their parentage difficult to assess accurately. The complexity is way outside the remit of this book; the genetic diversity of elms is the subject of international conservation efforts. In a final bid to make things less clear, Dutch Elm Disease has nothing to do specifically with the Dutch elm – it has that name because it was identified in Holland. Enough already?

Before you get overwhelmed with the botanics of it all, what does any of this mean when you look at the tree in Lewisham? Well, as with every tree, everything and nothing. That the tree has survived its difficult teenage years and has a potentially chequered lineage might actually give it a bit more interest than it otherwise deserves. Its location used to be a water meadow (the park is called Ladywell Fields, which indicates a watery provenance) and is now a corridor of green bisected by a railway and the fenced-in River Ravensbourne. A thin line between urban and suburban. The elm grows beside the river, behind a fence, among other trees and shrubbery. As you walk along the path, the branches that arch above belong to this elm – otherwise, you don't see it until you are right on top of its plaque. It has a slender, cylindrical trunk, splitting at around 12 feet, with tiny shoots coming off the trunk all the way up, making it look like a very hairy leg. To appreciate it, you need to walk backwards across the grass away from the elm – only from a good few yards away can you take in the whole tree and see how it towers above its fellows, like the child in a class who has had a growth spurt a few years before the others, and is self-consciously slumping in the back row of the school photo, in a vain attempt to fit in.

GETTING THERE

Map ⑫

Location Ladywell Fields, off Malyons Road, Lewisham, SE13.
Access The park is open from 8am to dusk.
Transport Ladywell rail/122, 284, 484, P4 bus.
Directions From Ladywell station, turn left and then second left into Malyons Road. Cross the river footbridge at the end of the road, and take the path to the right. The elm is directly ahead. A ten-minute walk in all.

The Dulwich Park Turkey Oak

Quercus cerris

You can tell much about a park by the quality of its signage. A provincial space might have 'no ball games', a gritty urban one, 'no alcohol'. In Dulwich Park there's a small, discreet sign proclaiming, joylessly, 'no golf practice'. Signs don't go up in parks willy-nilly, which suggests that this used to be a common venue for golf. It's no surprise; Dulwich is that kind of place.

Often with Great Trees in parks, you can wander around thinking 'is that the one?' about a good many of the beautiful specimens you pass, particularly in winter when there might be fewer distinguishing features. Then you come across the real thing, and there's no doubt. So it is in this park; fantastic trees abound, and then you come to this Turkey oak – a boldly magnificent tree, and a great example of the species, standing beside a driveway to the south of the park. Its growth suggests it has never been crowded: the huge solid bole has equally solid branches emanating from all sides, which in bare form gives it the spiky, rounded substance of a thick-spined hedgehog. The lowest branches grow so long and low as to be nearly touching the ground on one side; the other side tips up a little, giving it a quirky lopsided look like a seesaw not quite resting at centre. The Turkey oak is known for being a very fast, straight grower but this one doesn't quite fit that design: it seems to have bulked out as well as gone up. This may be because of its age, but it may have also contributed to its survival. There are no prizes for guessing the tree's country of origin. The Turkey oak was originally bought to England in the second half of the 19th century for timber – fast-growing trees mean faster-growing profits. However, the tree's timber shatters easily – ha! The tree has cleverly rendered itself purely decorative. This oak has a similar leaf to the classic English variety, but the lobes are longer and it's a darker green. Like all oaks it produces acorns, but this is where the Turkey oak really distinguishes itself: each cup of each acorn has a gorgeous set of whiskers, giving it the alternate name of mossy cup oak.

While you're in Dulwich Park, scout around for some of the ancient oaks that marked the boundaries of the fields it used to be. Lieutenant-Colonel JJ Sexby (*see p50* Ravenscourt Plane) worked on the park in the 1890s (as well as just about every Victorian park in London); he included an American garden in his layout, which featured a great stand of silver birches, planted to shade the noted collection of rhododendrons and azaleas. If those showy traditional flowers do it for you, time your visit to coincide with their appearance. Silver birches, of course, look gorgeous year round.

GETTING THERE

Map ⑬

Location Dulwich Park, College Road, Dulwich, SE21.
Access The park is open from 8am to dusk.
Transport West Dulwich rail/ P4, P13 bus.
Directions Turn right out of the station and walk along Dulwich Common. After about ten minutes, turn left into Dulwich Park through Queen Mary's Gate. Follow the path to the right towards the sports ground. The oak is a little further along, on the right.

QUERCUS
CERRIS
(TURKEY OAK)

The Greenwich Spanish Sweet Chestnut

Castanea sativa

Greenwich was a centre of creative Restoration activity in the 1660s. Charles II had come back from exile in France full of enthusiasm for the large-scale garden design of the celebrated André Le Nôtre, responsible for the Palace of Versailles. Charles asked Le Nôtre to design Greenwich Park in the same formal style, which included geometric precision, vistas and avenues. The Greenwich acreage, which has had Celt and Roman residents, had been enclosed in 1433 and used mainly as royal hunting and pleasure grounds. Le Nôtre designed for it a (never-completed) parterre – a formal 'knot'-style garden with a tight pattern of low, edged beds – and Charles II, after Le Nôtre's style, built a diamond-shaped network of avenues and a series of grass terraces planted with hawthorn. Hundreds of new trees were planted.

At this time, John Evelyn was writing his 1664 opus, *Sylva: A Discourse of Forest Trees*, to encourage tree planting among landowners, thereby generating timber for the navy. He was the local expert, so probably advised on the planting of a plethora of sweet chestnuts, which had until then been planted only in forests. Thanks to Evelyn, Greenwich is host to one of the oldest forest trees planted in an English park.

And how glorious it is. A huge, twisting Goliath. Disproportionately wide-girthed, it is hollow and misshapen, the trunk looking in parts as if the bark has peeled in disdain from its own insides. About two feet up from the ground, the tree becomes a vibrant orange-brown. Deep, long rivers of fissure have developed a spiral twist, making the whole tree look as if it's revolving on its roots to see what goes on round the corner. The contorted shape gives it a tortured look – which is all an act.

It has cavities and splits, the evidence of early pollarding now hollowing out. As you walk around the tree, the trunk presents different faces, different colours, different textures, as if a gathering of lesser trunks were baled together to create one super-trunk. If you've ever seen wool under a microscope, you've seen the same look. This great, buttressed thickness extends nearly to the crown of the tree, where it breaks into foreshortened fat arms. All these things are entirely in accordance with the tree's age; it's doing exactly what it should. And that includes providing an excellent refuge for wildlife: the splits provide handy niches for insects and fungi, and fine roosting spots for bats, while the vertical cavities become a bench for an elderly pigeon or two.

The historic sweet chestnuts from this tree are prized locally (do 'Great' chestnuts taste sweeter?), though Greenwich residents might not appreciate the comments of Evelyn, that 'we might propagate their use among our common people, being a food so cheap and so lasting.'

GETTING THERE

Map ㊹

Location Flower Garden, south-east corner of Greenwich Park, Greenwich, SE10 8QY. The nearest entrance is Blackheath Gate on Charlton Way.
Access The park is open from 6am until just after dark.
Transport Greenwich rail/DLR/ Blackheath rail/188 bus.
Directions From Greenwich station, it's a 40-minute walk. Follow signs for the Royal Observatory. From there, head south down Blackheath Avenue and left into the Flower Garden. Take the right fork, and follow the path as it curves left. The chestnut is 20 yards past the bend on the left-hand side.

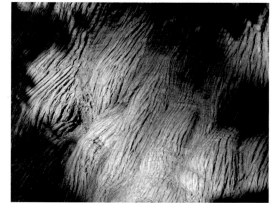

The Greenwich Park Shagbark Hickory

Carya ovata

Greenwich Park is monumentally packed; literally, packed with monuments. It's got history, royalty, art and architecture on an enviable scale; it's got a view of London at its feet. It's even got time. It's a Grade-I listed landscape, and a Site of Metropolitan Importance for Nature Conservation, replete with wildlife of considerable relevance. It's the kind of place where you can imagine even the worms having special preservation status. So be careful where you tread.

That is quite some build-up, a context in which to expect greatness. This tree had better be something extraordinary. Actually, it's a rather delicate-looking interloper in a landscape of enormity. It may be the largest shagbark hickory in the country, but it remains an upright southern belle in a room of fattened old crones. It stands discreetly on a corner of the Flower Garden, an enclosed part of the park full of winding paths, formally planted circular flower beds and a large duck pond. Growing tall and narrow, and sparingly branched, the tree is rather hidden because it doesn't have the girth of the trees around it. But what it lacks in stance it makes up for in its bark, performing, as its name requires, by being good and shaggy. Covering a narrow greyish bole, the bark is an overlapping mosaic of long, thin platelets, each one peeling at the top and bottom. It looks as if you could shake the trunk vigorously and all the excess bark would fall off in a great dry dandruff rustle. This gives it a sense of fragility.

The tree is grown as an ornamental in this country, and has been since the 1620s. It's not grown just for its bark, which gives the tree very good winter appeal; it also has splendid autumnal colour, with leaves turning a true gold. In late spring, this monoecious tree has male flowers appearing as catkins and females as tiny green spikes. In its native eastern United States, it's not just a pretty face but is a well-used commercial tree. It has a very hard, dense wood, which is ideal for fuel and is used extensively in the world of making and doing, from ladders to baseball bats (in the early days of the sport, at least – Babe Ruth used one, but hickory bats are considered too heavy now). Unparalleled strength in a world of wood! The trees produce a syrup much like the more famous maple. And being a member of the walnut family, it has an edible nut – though there wouldn't be enough on this one tree to warrant calling it a harvest. The shagbark nut is considered the best of the hickory nuts, and has quite a specialised market. It was a crucial tree to Native Americans (the word hickory comes from the Algonquin peoples, who used the nut's oily fat as a valuable foodstuff). And the fragrance of the wood smoke makes it a popular choice for curing ham and bacon. So it's known for its bark and its bite.

GETTING THERE

Map 45

Location Flower Garden, south-east corner of Greenwich Park, Greenwich, SE10 8QY. The nearest entrance is Blackheath Gate on Charlton Way.
Access The park is open from 6am until just after dark.
Transport Greenwich rail/DLR/Blackheath rail/188 bus.
Directions From Greenwich station, it's a 40-minute walk. Follow signs for the Royal Observatory. From there, head south down Blackheath Avenue and left into the Flower Garden. Where the path forks, the tree lies straight ahead between the two routes, in front of the holly trees.

The Charlton House Mulberry

Morus nigra

Be full of historical reverence when you view this tree and verily you shall be rewarded. The story is rich with royal good intent, and it has a nice ending.

King James I, who ruled England from 1603 until his death 22 years later, had a stance on smoking that can only be described as unambiguous: 'A custom loathsome to the eye, hateful to the nose, harmful to the brain, dangerous to the lungs.' He was so anti-smoking, he ordered the planting of thousands of mulberry trees in the American state of Virginia, then part of the English Crown, in an attempt to crowd out tobacco planting. As we know, he lost. Cigarettes won.

But it's clear that James was a big fan of the mulberry tree. Deciding that Britain needed its own silk industry in the early 1600s, he issued edicts on their planting, as they were the food supply of silkworms. Masses of mulberries were planted across the country; even his friend William Shakespeare grew one. The king made payments of 'the sum of L. (Pounds Sterling) 935 for the charge of four acres of land taken in for His Majesty's use, near to his Palace of Westminster, for the planting of Mulberry trees.' His mistake was simple, but costly. It's the white mulberry that feeds the silkworm, and he ordered the planting of the black mulberry, *Morus nigra*. Which brings us to Charlton, paying homage to a tree so distinguished it is featured on 'great trees' lists that cover specimens across Britain.

It's disputed whether this mulberry, planted in 1601, is the oldest in the country, however. Several other contenders claim an extra 50 years or so. It definitely looks old. It looks exhausted – but it's not: the tree fruits prolifically enough for mulberry jam to be a local offering. Now almost completely recumbent, the tree has floppy, relaxed limbs. What was once a central trunk is now divided into long branches providing a low, bowl-like frame. In this almost horizontal state, height isn't relevant, but these are not trees grown for height, 40 feet being usual. The trunk, splayed as it is, pierces the iron fencing around it in several places, suggesting it has settled gently into this new pose over the years. The old growth is gnarled and split – these trees grow slowly, so the trunk has an intricate fissure pattern along with larger splits, twists and holes. The newer growth is smoother, with whip-like shoots. After the pink blossom comes the fruit, resembling fat, stretched-out raspberries, which drop from the tree when ripe, and so must be gathered from the ground.

The ending brings us full circle: a cutting from this tree was taken in the winter of 2008 to plant at the site of James I's original mulberry garden in the grounds of Buckingham Palace. If you have aspirations, you can buy a tree grown from cuttings from the Charlton House Mulberry, and boil up your own version of royal jam.

GETTING THERE

Map 46

Location Grounds of Charlton House, Charlton Road, SE7 8RE.
Access The park is open from 8.30am to dusk.
Transport Charlton rail/53, 54, 380, 422 bus.
Directions A ten-minute walk uphill from the station. Exit right and up Charlton Church Lane. At the top of the hill, take the right-hand fork and almost immediately cross over Charlton Road into Charlton Park. The mulberry is behind a red-brick toilet block, ten yards from the entrance, on the left.

The Bexley Charter Oak

Quercus robur

When you hear that this old oak was the site of the signing of a charter, you start to imagine marvellous things. A great charter under a great tree – what a scene! Men in velvet breeches and shoes with buckles, wielding quills with a flurry of pomp and the toss of a curly white wig. Lute music. A charter conjures up historical shenanigans freeing people from shackles; it suggests human rights and abolitions and majestic statements. A declaration, maybe, freeing the people of Bexley from poverty and serfdom? Allowing them to graze their sheep in perpetuity? The reality is rather more humdrum: the charter signed under this great old tree was issued in 1937, which is definitely past the time when white wigs were worn for anything other than judicial matters or TV costume dramas. It's even harder to get excited about this charter when you discover that it changed the designation of Bexley from an urban district council, to a municipal borough. Be still your beating heart, and put away the bunting.

Once you're beyond that set of expectations, this tree is exactly what an old oak, a common *Quercus robur*, should look like. It's now well over 200 years old, and it stands alone, so it must have been planted with the expectation that it would always make an impressive specimen. In that sense, it's done its bit. It's set in the middle of a huge grass space that slopes gently down from a square yellow house to a lake; on a lucky day, Canada geese will strut along two by two, to complete the scenario perfectly. The tree has a huge spread exactly encircled by a wide fence, aimed at increasing its moisture take-up and protecting the delicate root system, but stopping you from any tree-hugging predilections. It has a gorgeous shape and a thick trunk, and has been well maintained. On one side a major branch has been removed, opening the view under the canopy of the tree, and providing an opportunity to see the fullness of the trunk – as if it was lifting its old skirts to give you a proper look at what is holding the whole thing up. It's much wider than it is tall, and brings to mind those outfits that ladies wore when multi-layered bustles and petticoats meant they had to walk through doorways sideways.

It's too simplistic to describe Danson House as a square yellow house, however. It's actually a Grade-I listed villa built in Palladian style in the mid 1760s. It fell into disrepair in the 20th century. After 35 years of neglect, English Heritage began a ten-year restoration. In 2005, the house reopened, and has restricted public viewing between April and October. The design of the estate is attributed to Capability Brown, who gave the original owner his own massive lake. The lake is still there, but was presumably even nicer when this was a quiet outpost; if you stand still and admire the view, you can hear (but not see) the relentless hum of distant traffic, giving the air that distinctive suburban feel.

GETTING THERE

Map ㊼

Location Danson Park, Danson Road, Bexleyheath, DA6 8HL.

Access The park gates are open from 7.30am Mon-Fri, 9am Sat, Sun, and close at sunset, or at 4.30pm in winter.

Transport Bexleyheath rail/ 89, 486, B14, B16 bus.

Directions Turn right out of the station, then left into Avenue Road. At Crook Log Broadway, turn right. Head over the mini roundabout, then turn left into Danson Road. Go past the main entrance to Danson Park and instead enter by the gate opposite Bean Road. The oak is visible ahead, slightly to the left, standing between the lake and Danson House, and surrounded by a circular iron fence.

The Morden Cemetery Horse Chestnut 🍃

Aesculus hippocastanum

Modern sensibilities tell us that it's a little strange to go on a tree hunt in a burial place; in our sophistication, we prefer to hide death away, protect ourselves from the inevitable. But our Victorian precursors didn't feel the same way; it was a time of grand mourning, of dramatic garb and statuary, of massive processions. From the 1830s, London saw the building of all its major cemeteries, and they became social places, somewhere to go out for the day, promenading among the laid-out gardens, graves and mausoleums.

When you come to this tree, death is all around, no two ways about it. And when you look at the tree, you'll see that life is also in rude abundance. Aged around 100, its planting ties in to the opening date of the cemetery in 1891. And, actually, it's two trees, one single-stemmed and one twin-stemmed, growing close enough to create one canopy. Their growth pattern has made them distinctive – branches have drooped downwards, sweeping along the floor and then rising up again, creating a protective set of branch bayonets around the trunks. At the time of writing, there are tiny horse chestnut shoots like upright nails all over the floor beneath the canopy, each bearing the sticky cola sweet of a leaf bud. Some of the branches have been lying across the floor long enough to have taken root. It happens. That could explain these tiny shoots, which might be suckers growing out from the new root systems, or perhaps regeneration from scattered conkers. To be definitive would mean digging up around the new shoots, which could be pointlessly damaging.

Morden Cemetery is also home to some of the best neutral grassland in the London area, which is more interesting than the name suggests. Here, it's apparently reminiscent of traditional meadowland that would have had occasional grazing, and as this used to be farmland, that jigsaw piece fits well. This kind of grassland is very important for biodiversity, and the site is home to black knapseed, ox-eye daisies, vetchlings, vetches and loads of butterflies. It became horticulturally 'famous' for its green winged orchids, although they haven't been spotted recently. They were first seen here in 1979, flowering tremendously; and while they're not terribly rare, they are protected in some places. The species is in decline in the south-east, so their non-appearance here might be part of that bigger picture.

If the more formal areas of the cemetery were not carefully tended to, they would also revert to neutral grassland. In the height of summer, it's a great sight: tall grasses, bright and beautiful wildflowers, masses of insects and butterflies – the rolling countryside of our imagination, right here in suburban Morden.

GETTING THERE

Map 49

Location Morden Cemetery, Motspur Park, SM4 4NU.
Access The cemetery is open from 8am (10am Sun) and closes at dusk.
Transport Motspur Park rail/ 163, 293, 413 bus.
Directions From the train station, exit left and follow Station Road around a right-hand bend. Head straight over Barnes Lane into Marina Avenue, and into the playing fields. Keep to the left and take the gate into the cemetery. Walk straight ahead; the chestnut is behind the chapel on the left. It's a 15- to 20-minute walk from the station.

The Morden Cemetery Horse Chestnut

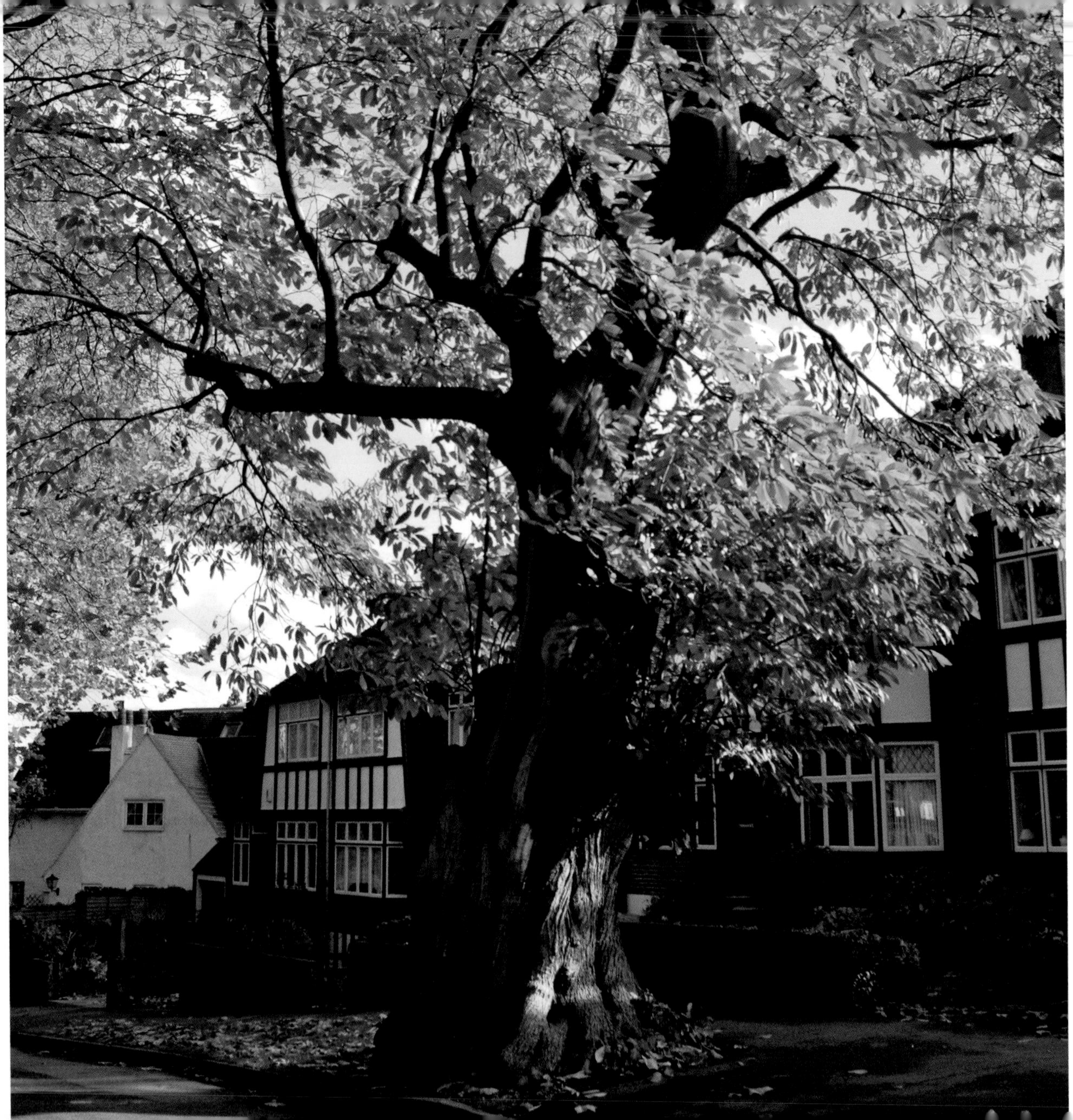

The Ashcombe Sweet Chestnut

The Ashcombe Sweet Chestnut 🌿

Castanea sativa

Around 50 short paces away from the Carshalton Sweet Chestnut (*see p188*), but cruelly exiled from the safety of Carshalton Park, lies the Ashcombe sweet chestnut. Does this one suffer from being compared to the Carshalton tree? Yes. Is it a fabulous tree in it's own right? Well (sigh), it's not bad. If you're going to see one, you might as well see both. And 'buy one, get one free' is as good an offer as this tree might ever get.

The problem is, the sweet chestnut is not a great street tree; it doesn't fulfil the right set of requirements. They grow fat and lumpen rather than tall and shading. They are unpredictable and individual, and so are never going to carry off that 'neat line' look. This one looks as out of place as a hippo trying to hide in a troupe of dancing gazelles. Actually, there are several sweet chestnuts on Ashcombe Road as it follows the park boundary on two sides; they're about as old as the ones inside the railings. At which point, scales fall from eyes, and reasons become clear: these trees started life inside the park, which is now a tenth of its original size. (A surviving part of the boundary wall can be seen to the rear of Ashcombe Road.) The fact that the road is distinctly suburban adds to the incongruity, because, in their aged state, with all those holes and cavities and craggy bits, these trees reek history, not suburbia. But this tree was never intended for street life; it's the tree that has been badly served by people, rather than the tree badly serving its location. Poor tree – once nurtured in the bosom of its ancient woody family, now shut out to live as a displaced street specimen.

Actually, it's better to view this as a great trunk, rather than a great tree, because that avoids dwelling on lost potential. On those terms, it's doing fine, because the trunk displays the features of a sweet chestnut very well, albeit in pruned form. The twisting motion that mature chestnuts have is really pronounced right across the whole tree in this shortened state. By nature, this is a tree that goes out rather than up, getting fatter and more squat as it ages; this one is very wide for its height, which means it's pushing its luck in terms of pavement space at the base. It has been cut according to the needs of the roadside location, losing one huge main branch that would otherwise lean dangerously across the traffic. The three main pollards show how it has lost its symmetry, leaving it with an interesting leaning curve. Old bark has stripped from some of the trunk, to make it very textural. On the pavement side, amid all the whip shoots, lopped-off bits and fissures is a lovely round hole, perfect for a little owl.

GETTING THERE

Map 49

Location Outside 45 Ashcombe Road, Carshalton, SM5.
Access On a public road and accessible at all times.
Transport Carshalton Beeches rail/127, 157, 407, X26 bus.
Directions Turn right out of the station into Gordon Road. Head to the end of the road, turn left into Glebe Road, then right into Grosvenor Avenue. Take the next left into Park Avenue, then left again into Ashcombe Road. The tree is 30 yards ahead, outside house no.45.

The Carshalton Sweet Chestnut

Castanea sativa

On a cool January morning, the Hog Pit looked less than impressive, but the site of Carshalton Park's annual bonfire and fireworks display had obviously inspired an optimistic fire-starter. A smoking wooden pallet that was never, on this damp day, going to be an exciting blaze, greeted anyone venturing into the park. Glamorous, it was not. But it was a timely reminder of why the Carshalton sweet chestnut is locally known as a 'miracle' tree.

The Hog Pit is a round, deep indentation near the north entrance of the park, not unlike the kind of bowl that alien landings create in movies. Its exact origins are unclear – it may have been an early pond or quarry. To call it an amphitheatre is to be kind. But it has survived centuries to become what looks like the perfect location for teenage BMX bikers to break a limb or two. If you're visiting on your bike, be sure to enjoy a few laps of it. Then, skirt to the right and head south, up the hill, to where the sweet chestnut, one of five in the park, hugs the boundary railing.

This miracle tree is so-called because it has survived serious arson attacks, with fire taking advantage of the hollows around the base to rip through its centre. The solution has been to block off these hollows by means of a little wooden door. This addition has been charmingly handled – it's natural, rustic and chunky. You'd have to be a hardened cynic not to want to open the door (you can pull it a few inches to peep inside), and the stories are all there, waiting to be told, about what – or who – lies behind, giving the tree even more character than nature and age provided.

The tree is around 400 years old, planted when this was a deer park ten times its current size. In 1892, the owners sold off part of it for housing. The tree was planted to provide food for livestock, and now it feeds woodworm, lichen, fungi and moss: a supermarket for micro beasts. It's a twisting, vibrant, many-featured thing. Where it has been cut, the remaining stump of an individual branch would have been bigger than a lot of trees in their entirety. Its girth is huge – and in common with other sweet chestnuts, the main bole is ridged and rounded to look like several trunks wrapped in one. The oldest part of the tree has fissures running deeply up the bark. It's green and mossy where the sun hits least, and a dark browny-orange on the other side – and very tactile. Further up, newer branches spring from the old, and their bark is as smooth and light as youth – trees grow on trees on trees. Interesting shapes have been hollowed out of the old wood; from every angle there are cavities and pockets created from curious twists and growth patterns. On one side of the tree, the outer bark has peeled back, and the tree, unarmoured, reveals its inside self – here, you can see the wood from the tree.

GETTING THERE

Map 50

Location West side of Carshalton Park, The Park, Carshalton, SM5.
Access The park gates are open from 8am to dusk.
Transport Carshalton Beeches rail/ 127, 157, 407, X26 bus.
Directions Turn right out of the station into Gordon Road. At the end, turn left into Glebe Road, then right into Grosvenor Avenue. Take the next left into Park Avenue, then left again into Ashcombe Road. Follow the railings left and around the corner; the sweet chestnut is 30 yards ahead, just inside the park boundary.

GREAT TREES OF LONDON
The Carshalton Chestnut
Castanea sativa
Awarded 18 November 2008
by Trees for Cities
www.treesforcities.org
Sponsored by Barratt Homes and Magic 105.4

The Carshalton Plane

Planatus x hispanica

In a pedantic mood? This tree has, like others in this book, been proclaimed one of the tallest planes in London, one of the tallest in England, and even one of the tallest in Europe. It could be all of those things, but this is probably an unwinnable point – unless there is someone out there with a highly developed sense of righteousness, a tape measure and a pair of thighs strong enough to shimmy up some very long trunks. Unquestionably, this is an enormous tree. And planted in a garden square or park with masses of space around it, you would be able to really appreciate its proportions. As it stands, however – surrounded by the clutter of hedges, small buildings, other trees, a narrow river at its base – all these things take something away from it. And then, and then: a distinctive bird call from right at the top of the tree makes you look up to the furthermost branches. You take a few steps back to get a proper view. The birds look so far away, becoming tiny dots up there… at which point the tree's stature becomes glorious.

This plane has a good crown shape, uniform and full; the branch structure is excellent. It has been left to grow with only minor evidence of shaping, so it really is in tip-top natural form. It shows off how the smaller branches almost droop when they're holding their fruit; and these branches twist and curl decoratively. Any more pronounced and they'd look contorted. Some of the upper trunk provides a textbook display of how the plates of bark fall off to create a mottled camouflage pattern; it leaves that vertical face with a smooth, shining appearance just right for sliding down once the summit has been claimed. In all, it's very attractive structurally, and still going strong at some 200 years old.

The distinctive call from the top of the tree might well come from a parakeet – large colonies of these exotic birds have spread all across south London. There may be a time when their raucous screech and bright green flash across the sky seems commonplace, but for now, they still seem like proper celebrities. There's no guarantee that one will make a personal appearance at this tree, but there are lots of other natural phenomena, as it's situated right beside an ecology centre, packed with activities and events. The tree is in a conservation area just off Carshalton Ponds, fed by the River Wandle, which informed early manufacturing industry in the area (if nature isn't enough, there are bags of heritage stuff). You'll be disappointed, though, if you use Thomas Fuller's *History of the Worthies of England,* published in 1662, as a guidebook: 'In Cash-Haulton especially,' he wrote, 'there be excellent trouts: so are there plenty of the best wall-nuts in the same place.' There's not.

GETTING THERE

Map ⑤

Location Outside the Sutton Ecology Centre, Festival Walk, next to Carshalton Ponds, Carshalton, SM5 3NY.
Access On a public footpath and accessible at all times.
Transport Carshalton rail/ 127, 157, 407, X26 bus.
Directions Turn right out of the station, down the slope, then left into West Street, following the signs to Sutton Ecology Centre. Opposite the water tower on your right, turn left into Festival Walk. The plane is outside the centre building.

The Bromley Oak

Quercus robur

A tree that started life right at the heart of a particularly ripe sort of action has seen its view get, frankly, dull. Once upon a time in Bromley, from about 400 years ago, this oak stood at the bottom of Love Lane, the local red-light district. Now, the activities under or near the tree might still provoke perspiration, but probably involve more Lycra, as Love Lane has become the entrance to a sports centre. One access route takes you through the Glades, an indoor shopping experience like all the other indoor shopping experiences. In the old days you might have seen some things to raise your eyebrow, but now, there's nothing to redeem the space the tree is in – unless you love the multi-lane road throbbing beside it, or the grimy plastic walkway just beyond, the sort of covered bridge that crosses motorways.

The tree is dark and erect, a fat trunk splitting low down into three solid branches going upwards but barely outwards, keeping a narrower profile than its species, *Quercus robur*, would suggest. Tree husbandry is very visible here; there has been lots of pollarding, which gives it a chopped-off, strait-jacketed look. From red light to Red Route: because it's on a main through-road, the tree is ruled by the ubiquitous two-headed gorgon of Health & Safety – managing the health of a bit of heritage while maintaining the safety of drivers. That is all very reasonable; no one wants their bus window poked in by a branch, even from a Great Tree. But the tree wears the corset of progress heavily; it has become a tree definitely curtailed by its position. There's little overhanging, nothing allowed to reach a 'natural' conclusion, nothing left to chance. However bleak that might sound, trees do have longevity on their side. This one has seen hundreds of years of progress – it may well outlive shopping and cars as a national pastime.

Actually, shopping has always featured in Bromley. A market has existed here for more than 800 years, one that caught the highest attention in the land. King John granted the market charter in 1205, to be held on a Tuesday. It was revised to Thursday in further decree from Henry VI. Between the market site and the Bromley Oak sits Queens Gardens, a charming, small formal park and also an important link in tracking the lineage of this tree. The gardens used to be part of the farmland belonging to Bromley Palace, which has existed in some form or other since the 1100s. In its current incarnation, it's the civic centre across the main road. This oak tree is historically recorded as a boundary tree. Put it all together, and the story of old Bromley comes into focus: the edge of the grand estate, the site of an important town market and, lest we forget, the entrance to Love Lane – 'you can't miss it, it's right by that big old oak tree', is phrase that was no doubt frequently uttered here in times past.

GETTING THERE

Map 52

Location East side of the Glades Shopping Centre, Kentish Way, Bromley, BR1 1DN.

Access On a public road and accessible at all times.

Transport Bromley South rail/ 208, 227, 261, 354, 358 bus.

Directions Turn right out of the station, then immediately right again. Head down the hill, then up a walkway. At the top of the steps, turn left into Kentish Way. About 200 yards ahead on the left you'll see the Pavilion Leisure Centre. The oak is just outside, before the footbridge.

THE BROMLEY OAK
ON THE SITE OF LOVE I...
ONE OF THE
GREAT TREES OF LONDO...

QUERCUS...

Branching out

Where to go in London for further aboreal inspiration.

London is bursting with places to see trees, and sometimes grasses and plants are part of the package, which isn't exactly a hardship. Some of the most special are personal – first dates, first thoughts, first steps. Trees are such great markers of occasions because we love to meet and sit under them. More and more of them are right up high – a few trees are well suited to roof gardens. 'Open garden' days are a perfect opportunity to get a nose in and see what individuals have done with their own space; and every year, London hosts **Open Garden Squares Weekend** (www.open squares.org), giving access to spaces normally closed to the public. There's the **Garden Museum** (www.gardenmuseum.org.uk), formerly the Museum of Garden History, next to Lambeth Palace and a garden in the **Barbican**'s conservatory. And of course there are the many **London parks** – public and royal, Victorian or otherwise – from Greenwich to Richmond, from the wilds of Hampstead Heath to the coiffed grounds of St James Park, that offer a mix of historic and contemporary vistas and fantastic, ever-expanding collections of trees… with the added bonus that they're free.

There are, however, a couple of exceptional spots in London that mustn't be missed for tree-lovers: Kew's Royal Botanic Gardens and the Chelsea Physic Garden.

Kew Gardens (www.kew.org) is magical. A place of plant conservation through science and research, it has massive botanical collections, glasshouses and stunning, seemingly endless lists of amazing trees, ranging from huge to tiny (the minutiae of a bonsai collection). The Rhizotron & Xstrata Walkway takes you right down under the roots of the trees, then up to a 59-foot-high canopy stroll that is a whole new perspective on life at the top. Seasonally adjusted guided tours are available, as are tree-identification tours. Or try one of the trails to see trees known specifically for their bark, and heritage tree tours celebrating the arboretum's unrivalled collection. It can be an educational visit if you choose, or you can lose yourself in the wonder of so many beautiful specimens.

More low-key than Kew, and mentioned in this book as a place where early experimenting with new trees took place, the **Chelsea Physic Garden** (www.chelseaphysicgarden.co.uk; *pictured below*) is a fantastic, nurturing, 'secret' place within the city. It began as an apothecaries' garden, and has an important role now with its advocation of natural medicine. The riverside location means it has a good microclimate that supports non-native trees, such as the largest outdoor fruiting olive in Britain. It's known more for its plants than trees, but is still a glorious retreat as the consumerism and cars that surround it get ever more blatant.

The Bromley Oak

The Downe Yew

Taxus baccata

'The sweetest place on earth', said Charles Darwin of St Mary's graveyard, which hosts this tree. Given his views on religion, the fact that he was generously able to say that makes it seem churlish to quibble that this isn't really London. And, since he described his house (which is just down the road) as 'at the extreme verge of the world', that suggests he would agree. To be at the edge of the world, and at the same time in London – the centre of everything – would be an impossibility.

You can't escape Darwin, unless you never evolved. But you certainly can't in Downe, and neither should you want to. The village is old and very pretty, and Darwin's house is the main tourist feature. Fortunately, the whole place has avoided being turned into a science-based theme park. Instead, it's discreet and charming, with small brown heritage signs pointing the way. A modest sundial on the church commemorates Darwin's 40 years in the place, and two of his children are buried in the churchyard.

The yew sits right at the edge of the church grounds. It's a beautiful little tree, with a perfect crown. This might lead you to expect that beneath it was a perfect trunk, but that isn't the case. In the darkness of the lower leaf and branch growth, the intricacies of the very wide trunk are hidden. As you approach, you can see how misshapen and broken it's become. Now it's an empty, split tube, providing a big hollow right through the trunk – you can walk through this tree. The almost-path makes it look as if it has actually evolved into two trees, one on either side of nothing. The remaining outer trunk is, yes, full of holes, but it's still solid; the branches either side of the empty tube are weighty with vigour. The colours are marvellous: masses of very dark green needle-leaves, the stout girth all oranges and modulated browns, flaky and rich. It's small but sumptuous, tempting and plumptious, like a fully stuffed tapestry cushion, exactly right for a village of proper pubs and hanging baskets and politeness.

The church dates from 1291, but the tree is almost definitely older than 700 years; there was Roman activity here before the church, and, as you can't count the rings in a hollow trunk, it's a job of comparing and contrasting. Another tree in this book tops 2,000 years, giving the Downe Yew hundreds of years to go. If you need somewhere to contemplate all that – time, religion, age, man – book a visit to Down House, Darwin's abode, and stride along his designated 'thinking path' – a sandy walkway where he could work out the problems of each day. You might be inspired to answer a few conundrums yourself. 'Can this really be London?' is a good starting point.

GETTING THERE

Map 53

Location Churchyard of St Mary the Virgin, High Street, Downe, Kent BR6 7UT.

Access The churchyard is open to the public from dawn to dusk.

Transport Bromley South rail then bus 146.

Directions From Bromley South station it's a 20-minute bus ride; alight at the village of Downe, then head south down the high street, past the Queens Head pub. The church is on your left and the yew is on the right as you enter the churchyard.

The West Wickham Oak

Quercus robur

Would it be a blessing or a curse to have a Great Tree in your own back garden? The West Wickham Oak stands at the end of a suburban garden, one branch reaching practically the whole length to the house. One has to wonder if clearing up historic acorns is a privilege or a pain? (Probably both.) Or if the possibility of visitors peering at the tree raises the pressure to keep your patio swept? The supplementary conundrum concerns the 'ownership' of trees, a nefarious subject at the best of times: at what point does a tree move from being 'yours' to 'ours'? And once a tree is listed, once it becomes officially important, do we all become temporary stakeholders? Can a custodian householder casually hang a netball hoop without holding a referendum?

There is a clear sense with this ancient tree that, actually, it doesn't sit at the end of a garden, the garden sits at the base of it. It positively exudes the sentiment 'you need to accommodate me'; the 'I was here first' defence. Indeed, the houses nearby do appear to have accommodated it. They've been built giving it due care and attention; rightly so, as they date from the 1920s to '40s, when this tree would have already been around 700 years old. It's barely aged since then. It sits amid rickety fences, a shabby wooden garage and a piece of patchy grass, with one side of the tree arching across and guarding that most valuable of London assets – a parking space. The bottom three feet of the trunk behind the fence is the only part not on public view. The oak definitely belies all the suburbanity around, bursting through the polite constraints of neatness. It is old, warm and brown. The bole is sumptuously fat and bubbled with old pollards. The branches are as big as trees in themselves, twisting and curling up, creating a crown that resembles mad old lady hair. West Wickham may not be the most dramatic resting place, but the tree has clearly been well cared for.

Quercus robur is also known as the pedunculate oak, because of its distinguishing feature: the acorns grow on a long peduncle, or stalk, while the leaves have only a short stalk. In sessile oaks, the other British native oak, that's reversed. They are very evocative trees, getting numerous mentions across the literary forms, and featuring in folklore not just in Britain, but among many early European tribes. Zeus, crowned with oak leaves, was said to speak through the medium of a sacred oak tree – a limited conversation, as it came via the rustling of leaves and cooing of doves in the branches. The Viking god Thor rode on an oak chariot, with a magic oak hammer. The revered oaks had power beyond the myths, however: during the Dark Ages, a common way of converting pagans to Christianity was to chop down their sacred oaks. It is our national tree, and that of America. And, yes, before you ask, we did get there first...

GETTING THERE

Map 54
Location Back garden of 2 Southcroft Avenue, West Wickham, Bromley, BR4 9JX.
Access On private land, visible over a fence.
Transport West Wickham rail/ 119, 194 bus.
Directions Leave the station by platform 1 exit. Turn left and left again into Station Road. Head all the way down Station Road until you reach the High Street; from here, cross straight over and head down Wickham Court Road. Turn right on to Woodland Way. The oak can be seen on the right, just after passing Aberdare Close on your left.

The Addington Palace Cedar of Lebanon 🌲

Cedrus libani

Any sentence that includes the words 'Six Archbishops' sounds either like the start of a bad joke, or the name of a real ale. This is neither. From 1807 to '89, the Palladian mansion Addington Palace was the official second residence of six successive archbishops of Canterbury. These days, Addington Palace is a venue for that soul-destroying couplet – corporate functions. There's a private golf club right beside it. Fortunately, the lovely view hasn't been privatised – it's a long sweep of green and trees interrupted only by the occasional mad shout of 'Fore!'.

The tree only pre-dates the archbishops by some three decades, but it must have pleased them, even as a thirtysomething. The species is referenced many times in the Bible, and the Lebanese origins would have made it highly apposite. Actually, it was trend not religion that led to the cedar's arrival here: the species was a necessary addition for the lawn of every fashionable estate from around 1760. Some of the first in the country were tried out in Chelsea Physic Garden in 1683 and they must have been quite the thing, being so distinctive in look. This one was part of the original landscaping from the 1770s, and is absolutely magical. Sited right behind the big house, you walk out the 'back door' and the end of an outstretched branch could practically poke you in the eye. The trunk is very broad in girth, and begins to split low down. On the ground beneath it are old branches long dead and parts of hollow trunk, some of it supine, some still erect. One main part of the trunk grows upwards to provide very high, scattered, flat platforms of green needles; the rest of the branches swoop really close to the ground, requiring now, in its senility, a lot of wooden props. One branch practically rattles the windows of the house, splitting into two flat umbrellas of pine just at head height. The props themselves, underpinning the lot, create a little maze of skeleton rooms right under the tree.

There may well be quite a few cedars of Lebanon in London's big estates and parks – and there are some jaw-dropping examples around – but it remains the kind of tree that, at its best, inspires a sharp intake of breath. And we're lucky this one is still here. It snowed in the early part of 2009 – two whole days of proper snow, the most we'd seen for decades. The weight of the snow brought down one major branch, and created topmost damage that, had it needed removal, would have affected the tree's majestic height. The surgery required post-snow actually opened up the tree, but the ropes round the area keeping people from wandering directly underneath the branches, show the levels of concern about this old wonder, obviously now in its dotage.

GETTING THERE

Map ⓹⓹

Location Grounds of Addington Palace, Gravel Hill, Addington, Surrey, CR0 5BB.

Access By arrangement, as grounds may be hired out for private functions (call 8662 5000).

Transport Gravel Hill tram/ 130, 466 bus.

Directions Leave the tram stop by the footbridge over the tracks, and enter the grounds of Addington Palace. Head along the driveway, passing the palace on the right. The tree is directly behind the house, with low, sprawling branches supported by large wooden props.

The Addington Palace Cedar of Lebanon

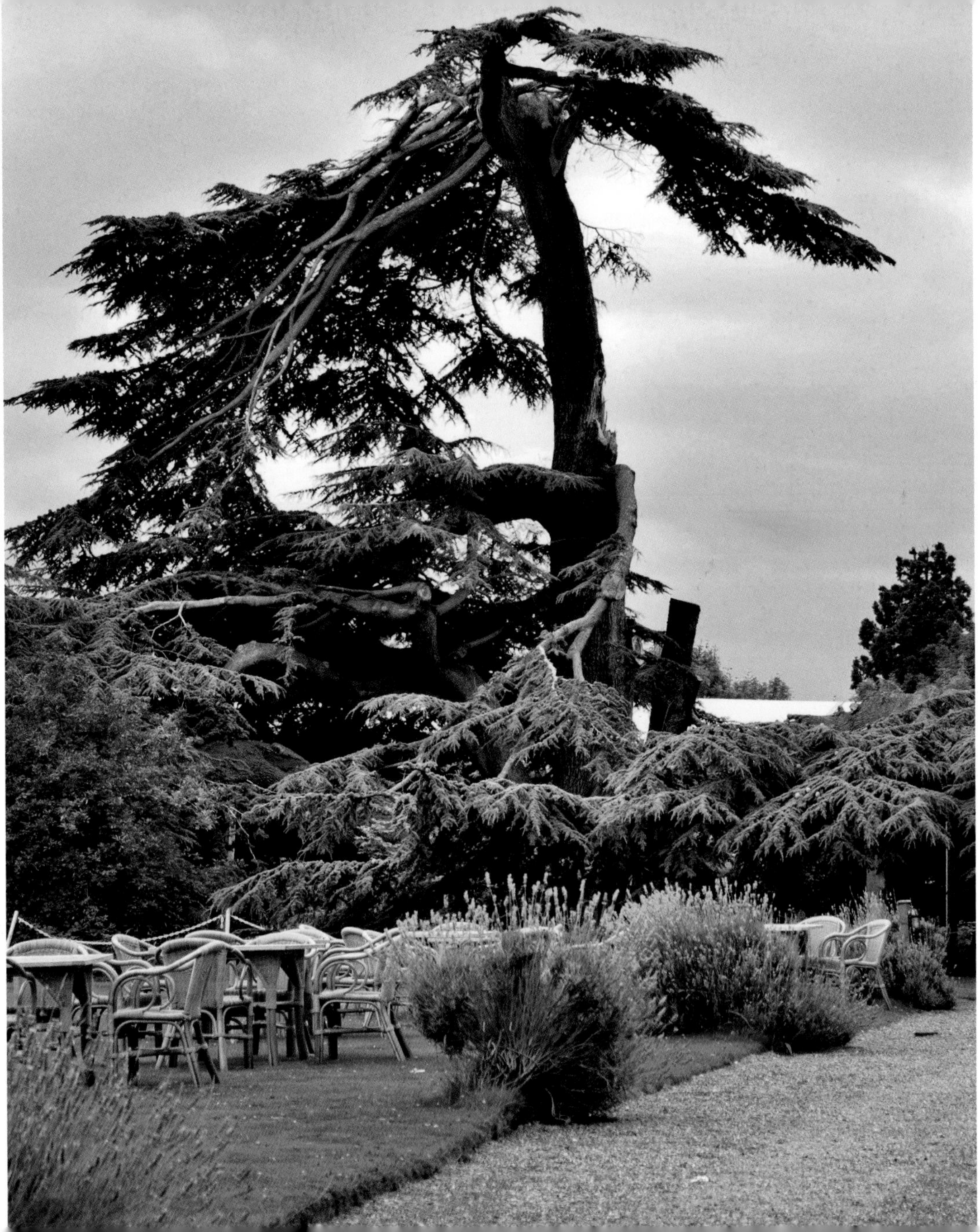

The Addington Palace Cedar of Lebanon

The Aperfield Cedar

The Aperfield Cedar

Cedrus libani

This looks like an enormous multi-trunked monster taking over a beautifully suburban front lawn. But that simple snapshot actually tells us quite a bit about the history of this area. In common with other huge trees that now find themselves dominating their surroundings, this cedar was here way before the surburbanisation of the area in the 1960s; it's simply not the kind of tree that would have been planted in this spot, at that time.

Long before it graced this front lawn and loomed over this teeny bungalow, the tree started life as part of the large estate of Aperfield Manor, land scattered with farms and cottages; it was probably near to the main house as it would have been a prestige landscape tree. In the 1830s, the estate was sold, and the owner, Frederick Dougal, parcelled much of it off into individual lots. By the early 1900s, plots of land here were for sale at ten pounds each, which seems a preposterously small amount, but those were the 'dud' sites on the hilliest bit of the old estate. Mostly people built small wooden houses not much grander than land-locked beach huts, and used them as weekend retreats. As time went on and the outer reaches of the city became more accessible and desirable for workers, the place became more populated. By the 1960s, the whole area of Biggin Hill and surrounds was seen as a suburb of London, and built and landscaped accordingly. Privet hedges – the quintessential symbol of the English ideal of being house proud – abounded. Seeing trees like this cedar, intended as huge specimens in massive acreage, really helps you to visualise how London would have looked around 200 years ago: a much smaller city ringed by massive houses luxuriously planted with trees we can now all treasure. An amazing amount of land in the ownership of a privileged few.

Like a lovely, friendly elephant politely sitting on a chair that is too small for it, all the blubbery bits spilling over, this tree is hanging on to the edge of the unsuitably small lawn, and both tree and lawn make their best effort to stay off the pavement without a restricting fence to stop them. The tree is unusual for a cedar in that the multitude of trunks all culminate at ground level, much more like the growth pattern of a shrub on steroids. A few large outer branches hold the shape of the tree at the base, and in the centre it's a jumble of giant pick-up sticks, an impenetrable circle of powerful branches pushing up. It towers above its surroundings, a fantastically shaped tree in very good condition. The many trunks have given it a much more rounded crown than old cedars often present. They can be interesting shapes: one or two solitary platforms of greenery up high, like twisted topiary, jagged and intensely constructed. With this one, each trunk culminates in a platform of green, and all together they merge to create a more solid round, an architecturally satisfying shape to the whole tree.

GETTING THERE

Map 56

Location Aperfield Road, Biggin Hill, Kent, TN16.

Access Just off a public road and accessible at all times.

Transport Bromley South, Bromley North or Hayes rail then 246 bus/New Addington tram then 464 bus.

Directions Alight from the 246 or 464 bus in Biggin Hill, just after Church Road (stop N). Go back and turn right down Church Road. The cedar is on the right, just after Village Green Avenue.

Gone but not forgotten

The Kingston Weeping Silver Lime ▼

Tilia petiolaris

Now just a big fat stump by the Thames in Kingston, on the path off the road. It is, however, nice to sit on – but beware of splinters if you do. The tree was removed, in that council phrase that's a gift for satirists everywhere, for 'health and safety reasons'.

The Barnsbury Beech ▲

Fagus sylvatica

This beech tree fell foul of a terminal fungus infection, the giant polyphore. A new tree was planted in the same spot in 2005.

The Crane Park Crack Willow ▼

Salix fragilis

This tree, next to the River Crane in Hounslow, was the largest crack willow in the country, but has now fallen over. The Latin name suggests it's fragile, and indeed it is.

The Kenley House Oak ▲

Quercus robur

A fantastic old tree that was originally in our selection for this book, but which is on private land and hidden from view.

◄ The Charlton House Nettle Tree

Celtis occidentalist

When the top half of the Charlton House Nettle Tree crashed on top of a lamppost and car in a storm in April 2002, the rest of the tree was discovered to be rotting, and was felled immediately.

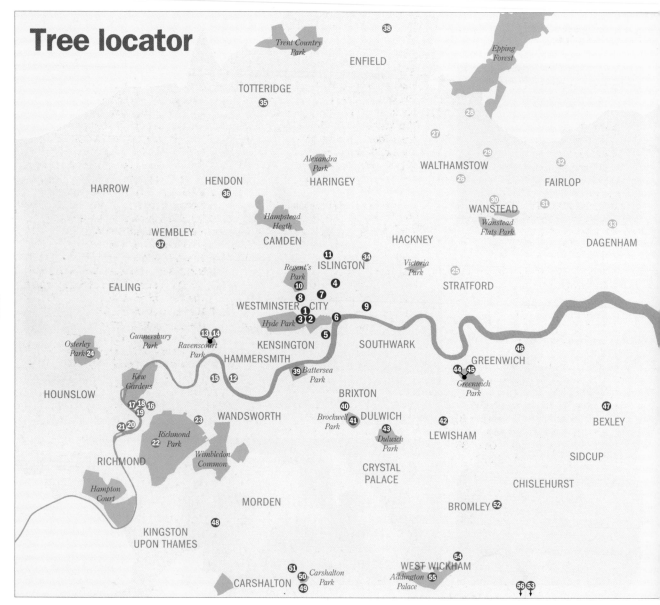

Tree locator

Trent Country Park

Epping Forest

38

ENFIELD

TOTTERIDGE

35

28

27

29

Alexandra Park

WALTHAMSTOW

32

HARROW

HENDON

HARINGEY

26

FAIRLOP

36

WANSTEAD

30

31

WEMBLEY

Hampstead Heath

CAMDEN

HACKNEY

Wanstead Flats Park

33

37

DAGENHAM

11 34

EALING

Regent's Park

ISLINGTON

Victoria Park

STRATFORD

10

25

4

8 7

WESTMINSTER CITY

9

1

6

3 2

Hyde Park

5

13 14

Gunnersbury Park

Osterley Park 24

Ravenscourt Park

KENSINGTON

SOUTHWARK

46

HAMMERSMITH

GREENWICH

39 Battersea Park

44 45

15 12

Greenwich Park

HOUNSLOW

Kew Gardens

BRIXTON

47

17 18 16

BEXLEY

19

40

DULWICH

21 20

23

Brockwell Park 41

42

RICHMOND

Richmond Park

22

43

LEWISHAM

Dulwich Park

SIDCUP

Wimbledon Common

CRYSTAL PALACE

CHISLEHURST

Hampton Court

MORDEN

BROMLEY 52

48

KINGSTON UPON THAMES

54

WEST WICKHAM

51 Carshalton Park

50

Addington Palace 55

CARSHALTON

49

56 53

MAP KEY

CENTRAL
❶ The Berkeley Plane p12
❷ The St James's Indian
  Bean Tree p16
❸ The Dorchester Plane p20
❹ The Brunswick Plane p24
❺ The Abbey Plane p28
❻ The Embankment Plane p30
❼ The Gower Plane p32
❽ The Marylebone Plane p34
❾ The Cheapside Plane p36
❿ The Regent's Plane p38
⓫ The Hardy Ash p42

WEST
⓬ The Fulham Palace Oak p46
⓭ The Ravenscourt Plane p50
⓮ The Ravenscourt Park Tree
  of Heaven p54
⓯ The Barn Elms Plane p58
⓰ The Black Horse Pollard
  Chestnut p62
⓱ The Asgill House Copper Beech p66
⓲ The Maids of Honour Stone Pine p68
⓳ The Riverside Plane p72
⓴ The Marble Hill Black Walnut p76
㉑ The York House Cut Leaf Beech p80
㉒ The Richmond Royal Oak p84
㉓ The Roehampton Lucombe Oak p88
㉔ The Osterley Park Cork Oak p90

EAST
㉕ The Stratford Fig p94
㉖ The Wood Street Horse
  Chestnut p98
㉗ The North Circular Cork Oak p102
㉘ The Friday Hill Plane p104
㉙ The South Woodford
  Copper Beech p108
㉚ The George Green Sweet
  Chestnut p112
㉛ The Valentines Park Maple p116
㉜ The Fairlop Oak p120
㉝ The Valence Park Oak p122

NORTH
㉞ The Amwell Fig p126
㉟ The Totteridge Yew p130
㊱ The Hendon Japanese Maple p134
㊲ The Wembley Elm p138
㊳ The Forty Hall Cedar of Lebanon p140

SOUTH
㊴ The Battersea Park Hybrid
  Strawberry Tree p148
㊵ The Tate Plane p152
㊶ The Brockwell Oak p154
㊷ The Lewisham Dutch Elm p158
㊸ The Dulwich Park Oak p160
㊹ The Greenwich Spanish
  Sweet Chestnut p164
㊺ The Greenwich Park Shagbark
  Hickory p168
㊻ The Charlton House Mulberry p172
㊼ The Bexley Charter Oak p176
㊽ The Morden Cemetery Horse
  Chestnut p180
㊾ The Ashcombe Sweet Chestnut p184
㊿ The Carshalton Sweet Chestnut p188
The Carshalton Plane p192
The Bromley Oak p196
The Downe Yew p200
The West Wickham Oak p202
The Addington Palace Cedar p206
The Aperfield Cedar p210

MAP

Glossary

A note on tree names.

All plants and trees are classified with Latin names under an internationally recognised binomial system that starts big, with the genus, then narrows to species. It can then subdivide further if the tree is a hybrid, variety or cultivar. Family comes first, but family names aren't generally recognised within the naming system because they're so broad. Every plant or tree has at least two parts to its identity (genus and species), hence binomial.

Allelopathy
The effect of one plant on another via the biochemicals the plant produces. The effect can be either beneficial or detrimental, depending on the plants involved.

Bifurcate
The splitting of a main body (a trunk, in this book) into two parts.

Bole
Another word for the trunk of a tree.

Catkin
The hanging spike of tiny flowers.

Chimaera
A plant composed of two or more genetically different tissues; a hybrid either by graft or mutation.

Compound leaf
A leaf that has separate parts but which is still definable as one thing (a rowan leaf, for example), as opposed to a simple leaf (as on a beech tree).

Cultivar
Short for 'cultivated variety'. An artificially created plant with distinct characteristics.

Dioecious
Bearing male and female flowers on separate plants; both types must be grown so that the plant can produce fruit.

Genus
The primary category in classification, under 'family' and above 'species'. Trees with similar characteristics share the first part of their Latin name (thus all oaks are *Quercus*) and are then further identified by species, as in *robur* or *ilex*.

Hybrid

A natural or artifical cross between parents from different genus or species. It's usually denoted with an 'x', as in *Platanus x hispanica* (*pictured right*).

Juglone

An allelopathic (*see above*) compound, synthesised by one plant to affect the growth of another.

Leaflet

A leaf-like segment or lobe of a leaf.

Lobe

A division of a leaf.

Monoecious

Bearing male and female flowers on the same plant.

Native

Occurring naturally; not known to have been introduced. *See p144-146* **British native trees**.

Palmate

Compound leaves (*see p218*) that are arranged around one shoot, like fingers on the palm of a hand. The horse chestnut is a good example (*pictured above left*).

Panicle

Where stalks of small individual flowers radiate from one stem, which itself can be branched or not. Lots of tiny flowers can make up one shape.

Pathogen

An agent that causes disease. Normally fungal, viral or bacterial in the case of trees.

Photosynthesis

The complex chemical reaction, whereby plants use the energy from light to produce food, taking in carbon dioxide and water and converting them to sugars and oxygen.

Pinnate

Leaflets (*see above*) arranged opposite each other along one leaf stalk – as on a yew.

Pollarding

A method of pruning trees to control growth. *See p41* **Pollarding**.

Samara

A simple, dry, winged fruit.

Species

The next layer of division after genus: the second part of the Latin name, such as *robur* or *fragilis*. Species breed true in the wild.

Variety

A subdivision of a species. Usually denoted by 'var.'.

Index

Index

Index

Index

Index